Reveling

THROUGH

REVELATION

Part II—Chapters 12-22

by

J. VERNON McGEE, Th.D., LL.D.

THRU THE BIBLE BOOKS
Box 100
Pasadena, California 91109

First Printing, May 1962
Sixth Printing, September 1974
Seventh Printing, September 1979
Eighth Printing, December 1979

FOREWORD

This second and final volume of notes on Revelation is a continuation of the series on the last chapters of the Revelation—chapters 12 through 22.

The primary purpose of these notes was to enable the listener to follow the series of lectures on the book of Revelation.

They have been placed in a more permanent and attractive form to make them available to a wider circle of folk who wish to study this great book on eschatology in the New Testament.

Though this work is not intended to be an elaborate or exhaustive treatment of Revelation, comments on each verse of every chapter are given to be helpful to the average student of prophecy.

The same method in presenting each verse is followed as in the preceding volume. The Authorized version is given so that the reader will not have to make continual reference to his Bible. In most cases the Authorized text is followed by a translation which we have made. This is added with the thought of getting as close to the original as possible.

We trust that this book will encourage many to seek the blessing that is promised to those who read, hear and keep those things which are written therein. May it quicken the hearts of believers into right expectation of the imminent coming of Christ for His Church.

INTRODUCTION

When the Pilgrims sailed for America, their pastor at Leyden reminded them, "The Lord has more truth yet to break forth from His Holy Word . . . . Luther and Calvin were great shining lights in their times, yet they penetrated not the whole counsel of God. . . . Be ready to receive whatever truth shall be made known to you from the written word of God." The 20th century has witnessed a renewed interest in eschatology (doctrine of last things), especially since World War I. Great strides have been made in the field of prophecy during the past two decades. Indeed new light has fallen upon this phase of Scripture. All of this attention has focused the light of deeper study on the book of Revelation.

In these brief notes we shall avoid the pitfalls of attempting to present something new and novel just for the sake of being different. Likewise, we shall steer clear of repeating threadbare cliches. Many works on Revelation are merely a carbon copy of other works.

By notes, comments, remarks, diagrams and word studies we shall attempt to get at the real meaning of the vision and symbols of Revelation.

There have been many approaches to this book, but these can be divided into four major systems. (Broadus lists 7 theories of interpretation, Tregelles lists 3.)

1. **Preterest Theory.** All of Revelation has been fulfilled in the past. It had to do with local references in John's day. It had to do with the days of either Nero or Domitian. This view was held by Renan and most German scholars, also by Elliott.

2. **Historical Theory.** Fulfillment of Revelation is going on in history, and Revelation is the prophetic history of the church, according to this theory.

3. **Historical-Spiritual Theory** is a refinement of the historical theory which was advanced by Sir William Ramsey. This theory states that the two beasts are Imperial and Provincial Rome. The point of the book is to encourage Christians. According to this theory, Revelation has been largely fulfilled and there are spiritual lessons for the church today. Amillennialism for the most part, has adopted this view. It dissipates and defeats the purpose of the book.

4. **Futurist Theory** holds that the book of Revelation is primarily prophetic and yet future, especially from Revelation 4 on to the end of the book. This is the view of all pre-millennialists and is the view which we accept and present.

SIX STRIKING AND SINGULAR FEATURES

1. It is the only prophetic book in the New Testament (in contrast to 17 prophetic books in the Old Testament).
2. John, the writer, reaches farther back into eternity past than any other writer in Scripture (John 1:1-3). He reaches farther on into eternity future in the book of Revelation.

3. Special blessing is promised the readers of this book (Revelation 1:3). Likewise, a warning is issued to those who tamper with its contents (Revelation 22:18, 19).

4. Revelation is not a sealed book (Revelation 22:10). Contrast Daniel 12:9. It is a revelation (apocalypse), which is an unveiling.

5. It is a series of visions, expressed in symbols.

6. This book is like a great union station where the great trunk lines of prophecy come in from other portions of Scripture. Revelation does not originate but consumates. It is imperative to a right understanding of the book to be able to trace each great subject of prophecy from the first reference to the terminal. There are at least 10 great subjects of prophecy which find their consummation here:

(1) The Lord Jesus Christ (Genesis 3:15).

(2) The Church (Matthew 16:18).

(3) The Resurrection and Translation of Saints (I Thes. 4:13-18; I Cor. 15:51, 52).

(4) The Great Tribulation (Deuteronomy 4:30, 31).

(5) Satan and Evil (Ezekiel 28:11-18).

(6) The "Man of Sin" (Ezekiel 28:1-10).

(7) The Course and End of Apostate Christendom (Daniel 2:31-45; Matthew 13).

(8) The Beginning, Course, and End of the "Times of the Gentiles" (Daniel 2:37; Luke 21:24).

(9) The Second Coming of Christ (Jude 14, 15).

(10) Israel's Covenants (Genesis 12:1-3), five things promised Israel.

REVELATION—APOCALYPSE

Key: Revelation 1:18-19

"Alpha—Omega"   "Things . . . seen"   "Beginning—End"

PAST	PRESENT	FUTURE
Son of Man In Heaven "I am he that liveth"	The 7 Churches "I was dead"	The Cosmic Crisis (After removal of true church and before the coming of Christ to creation)
"the things which thou hast seen"	"Behold, I am alive" "the things which are"	"I have the keys of hell and of death" "the things about to be after these things (meta tauta)"
Rev. 1	Rev. 2-3	Rev. 4-22
Christ in Glory	Church in the World	Crisis in the Future

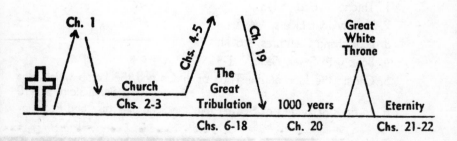

OUTLINE

I. The PERSON of Jesus Christ—Christ in Glory, chapter 1

A. Title of the Book, verse 1

B. Method of Revelation, verse 2

C. Beatitude of Bible Study, verse 3

D. Greetings from John the Writer, and from Jesus Christ in Heaven, verses 4-8

E. The Post-Incarnate Christ in a Glorified Body, Judging His Church (the Great High Priest in the Holy of Holies), verses 9-18
"we know him no longer after the flesh"

F. Time Division of the Contents of the Apocalypse, verse 19

G. Interpretation of the Seven Stars and Seven Lampstands, verse 20

II. The POSSESSION of Jesus Christ—The Church in the World, chaps. 2, 3

A. Letter of Christ to the Church in Ephesus, 2:1-7

B. Letter of Christ to the Church in Smyrna, 2:8-11

C. Letter of Christ to the Church in Pergamum, 2:12-17

D. Letter of Christ to the Church in Thyatira, 2:18-29

E. Letter of Christ to the Church in Sardis, 3:1-6

F. Letter of Christ to the Church in Philadelphia, 3:7-13

G. Letter of Christ to the Church in Laodicea, 3:14-22

III. The PROGRAM of Jesus Christ—The Scene in Heaven, chapters 4-22

A. The Church in Heaven with Christ, chapters 4-5

"I will come again, and receive you unto myself; that where I am, there ye may be also"

1. Throne of God, 4:1-3

2. Twenty-four Elders, 4:4, 5

3. Four Living Creatures, 4:6-11

4. Book with Seven Seals, 5:1-4

5. Christ: the Lion of the Tribe of Judah and the Lamb which Has Been Slain, 5:5-10

6. Myriads of Angels of Heaven Join the Song of Praise and Redemption, 5:11, 12

7. Universal Worship of the Saviour and Sovereign of the Universe, 5:13, 14

B. The Great Tribulation in the World, chapters 6-18

1. Opening of the **Seven-Sealed Book,** chapters 6-8:1
  a. Opening of the First Seal, 6:1, 2
    (Rider on a White Horse)
  b. Opening of the Second Seal, 6:3, 4
    (Rider on a Red Horse)
  c. Opening of the Third Seal, 6:5, 6
    (Rider on a Black Horse)
  d. Opening of the Fourth Seal, 6:7, 8
    (Rider on a Pale Horse)
  e. Opening of the Fifth Seal, 6:9-11
    (Prayer of the Martyred Remnant)
  f. Opening of the Sixth Seal, 6:12-17
    (The Day of Wrath Has Come—Beginning the Last Half of the Great Tribulation)
  g. Interlude, chapter 7
    (1). Reason for the Interlude Between the 6th and 7th Seals, 7:1-3
    (2). Remnant of Israel Sealed, 7:4-8
    (3). Redeemed Multitude of Gentiles, 7:9-17
  h. Opening of the Seventh Seal—Introduction of Seven Trumpets, 8:1

2. Blowing of the **Seven Trumpets,** chapters 8:2-11:19
  a. Angel at the Altar with Censer of Incense, 8:2-6
  b. First Trumpet—Trees Burnt, 8:7
  c. Second Trumpet—Seas Become Blood, 8:8, 9
  d. Third Trumpet—Fresh Water Becomes Bitter, 8:10, 11
  e. Fourth Trumpet—Sun, Moon, Stars Smitten, 8:12, 13
  f. Fifth Trumpet—Fallen Star and Plague of Locusts, 9:1-12
  g. Sixth Trumpet—Angels Loosed at River Euphrates, 9:13-21
  h. Interlude Between the Sixth and Seventh Trumpets, 10:1-11:14
    (1). The Strong Angel with the Little Book, 10:1-7
    (2). John Eats the Little Book, 10:8-11
    (3). Date for the Ending of "The Times of the Gentiles," 11:1, 2
    (4). Duration of the Prophesying of the Two Witnesses, 11:3-12
    (5). Doom of the Second Woe—Great Earthquake, 11:13, 14
  i. Seventh Trumpet—End of Great Tribulation and Opening of Temple in Heaven, 11:15-19

3. **Seven Performers** During the Great Tribulation, chapters 12-13
   a. The Woman—Israel, 12:1, 2
   b. The Red Dragon—Satan, 12:3, 4
   c. The Child of the Woman—Jesus Christ, 12:5, 6
   d. Michael, the Archangel, Wars with the Dragon, 12:7-12
   :. The Dragon Persecutes the Woman, 12:13-16
   f. Remnant of Israel, 12:17
   g. Wild Beast Out of the Sea—a Political Power and a Person, 13:1-10

   (1). Wild Beast, Description, verses 1, 2
   (2). Wild Beast, Death Dealing Stroke, verse 3
   (3). Wild Beast, Deity Assumed, verses 4, 5
   (4). Wild Beast, Defying God, verses 6-8
   (5). Wild Beast, Defiance Denied to Anyone, verses 9, 10

   h. Wild Beast Out of the Earth—a Religious Leader, 13:11-18
   (1). Wild Beast, Description, verse 11
   (2). Wild Beast, Delegated Authority, verses 12-14
   (3). Wild Beast, Delusion Perpetrated on the World, verses 15-17
   (4). Wild Beast, Designation, verse 18

4. **Looking to the End of the Great Tribulation,** chapter 14

   a. Picture of the Lamb with the 144,00, verses 1-5
   b. Proclamation of the Everlasting Gospel, verses 6, 7
   c. Pronouncement of Judgment on Babylon, verse 8
   d. Pronouncement of Judgment on Those Who Received the Mark of the Beast, verses 9-12
   e. Praise for Those Who Die in the Lord, verse 13
   f. Preview of Armageddon, verses 14-20

5. Pouring Out of the **Seven Mixing Bowls of Wrath,** chapters 15, 16

   a. Preparation for Final Judgment of the Great Tribulation, 15:1-16:1
   (1). Tribulation Saints in Heaven Worship God Because He is Holy and Just, 15:1-4
   (2). Temple of the Tabernacle Opened in Heaven that Seven Angels, Having Seven Golden Bowls, Might Proceed Forth, 15:5-16:1
   b. Pouring Out of the First Bowl, 16:2
   c. Pouring Out of the Second Bowl, 16:3
   d. Pouring Out of the Third Bowl, 16:4-7
   e. Pouring Out of the Fourth Bowl, 16:8, 9
   f. Pouring Out of the Fifth Bowl, 16:10, 11
   g. Pouring Out of the Sixth Bowl, 16:12

    h. Interlude: Kings of Inhabited Earth Proceed to Har-Magedon, 16:13-16

    i. Pouring Out of the Seventh Bowl, 16:17-21

  6. The **Two Babylons Judged,** chapters 17, 18

    a. The Apostate Church in the Great Tribulation, chapter 17

      (1). Great Harlot Riding the Wild Beast, verses 1-7

      (2). Wild Beast Destroys the Great Harlot, verses 8-18

    b. Political and Commercial Babylon Judged, chapter 18

      (1). Announcement of Fall of Commercial and Political Babylon, verses 1-8

      (2). Anguish in the World Because of Judgment on Babylon, verses 9-19

      (3). Anticipation of Joy in Heaven Because of Judgment on Babylon, verses 20-24

C. Marriage of the Lamb and Return of Christ in Judgment, chapter 19

  1. Four Hallelujahs, verses 1-6

  2. Bride of the Lamb and Marriage Supper, verses 7-10

  3. Return of Christ as King of Kings and Lord of Lords, verses 11-16

  4. Battle of Armageddon, verses 17, 18

  5. Hell Opened, verses 19-21

D. Millennium, chapter 20

  1. Satan Bound 1000 Years, verses 1-3

  2. Saints of the Great Tribulation Reign with Christ 1000 Years, verses 4-6

  3. Satan Loosed After 1000 Years, verses 7-9

  4. Satan Cast Into Lake of Fire and Brimstone, verse 10

  5. Setting of Great White Throne Where Lost Are Judged and Follow Satan Into Lake of Fire and Brimstone, verses 11-15

E. Entrance Into Eternity; Eternity Unveiled, chapters 21, 22

  1. New Heaven, New Earth, New Jerusalem, 21:1, 2

  2. New Era, 21:3-8

  3. New Jerusalem, Description of the Eternal Abode of the Bride, 21:9-21

  4. New Relationship—God Dwelling with Man, 21:22, 23

  5. New Center of the New Creation, 21:24-27

  6. River of the Water of Life and Tree of Life, 22:1-5

  7. Promise of Return of Christ, 22:6-16

  8. Final Invitation and Warning, 22:17-19

  9. Final Promise and Prayer, 22:20, 21

Chapter 12

THEME: The final conflict between Israel and Satan after he is cast out of heaven.

OUTLINE:

3. **Seven Performers** During the Great Tribulation, chapters 12-13
   a. The **Woman**—Israel, 12:1,2
   b. The Red **Dragon**—Satan, 12:3,4
   c. The **Child** of the Woman—Jesus Christ, 12:5,6
   d. **Michael,** the Archangel, Wars with the Dragon, 12:7-12
   e. The Dragon Persecutes the Woman, 12:13-16
   f. Remnant of Israel, 12:17

REMARKS:

Although the 7th Trumpet of chapter 11 brings us through the Great Tribulation and the Millennium to the very threshold of eternity, a great deal of detail was omitted. Beginning with chapter 12, this will be compensated for in the presentation of seven prominent personages who play a dominant part in the Great Tribulation period; the pouring out of the seven Bowls of Wrath; and the final destruction of Babylon.

The prominence of the nation Israel is brought before us (it was suggested in the previous chapter with the measuring of the temple on earth and the opening of the temple in heaven). The last verse (verse 19) of chapter 11 should be coupled with the opening of this chapter.

These 7 personages are representative of persons, both natural and supernatural, physical and spiritual, rulers and nations. The identification and clarification of these is essential for a proper understanding of the Revelation. A case in point is the woman with the man child, opening this section. Many expositors consider the identification of this woman the most important key to the understanding of the book of Revelation.

COMMENT:

a. The **WOMAN** —Israel (the first sign), verses 1,2

Verses 1, 2—And there appeared a great wonder in heaven; a woman clothed with the sun, and the moon under her feet, and upon her head a crown of twelve stars: and she being with child cried, travailing in birth, and pained to be delivered.

And a great sign was seen in heaven: a woman arrayed with the sun, and the moon under her feet, and upon her head a crown of twelve stars; and she was with child, and travailing in birth, and being tormented to be delivered.

The crux of the interpretation of the entire book of Revelation revolves about this point. Who is the woman? The heresy of Rome, which makes the woman represent the Virgin Mary, is well known. Unfortunately, many able expositors in the Protestant tradition did not depart from this method, but made instead the woman to represent the church of all ages. Practically all denominational literature follows this line.

1

Several female founders of cults have not been able to resist the temptation of seeing themselves pictured in this woman. Joanna Southcott said that she was the woman in Revelation 12, and in October, 1814 she would have the man child. This event never took place, yet her followers numbered up to 200,000 in the last century. Mrs. Mary Baker Eddy very modestly conceived the idea that she was the one pictured here. A female preacher in California, who became famous or infamous—however you care to express it—toyed with the idea that she might be the woman mentioned in this chapter.

We can dismiss all of these claims—unless we forsake all intelligent approach to the interpretation of Scripture.

The identifying marks of the woman are the sun, moon and stars. These belong to Israel, as seen in Joseph's dream:

> And he dreamed yet another dream, and told it his brethren, and said, Behold, I have dreamed a dream more; and, behold, the sun and the moon and the eleven stars made obeisance to me. And he told it to his father, and to his brethren: and his father rebuked him, and said unto him, What is this dream that thou hast dreamed? Shall I and thy mother and thy brethren indeed come to bow down ourselves to thee to the earth? (Gen. 37:9, 10).

The woman is a sign in heaven, though her career is on the earth. She is not a literal woman. The career of the woman corresponds to that of Israel. Israel gave birth to Christ, who is the child (verse 5).

> For unto us a child is born, unto us a son is given: and the government shall be upon his shoulder: and his name shall be called Wonderful, Counsellor, The mighty God, The everlasting Father, The Prince of Peace (Isa. 9:6).

> For it is evident that our Lord sprang out of Juda . . . (Heb. 7:14).

> Whose are the fathers, and of whom as concerning the flesh Christ came, who is over all, God blessed for ever. Amen (Rom. 9:5).

> But thou, Bethlehem Ephratah, though thou be little among the thousands of Judah, yet out of thee shall he come forth unto me that is to be ruler in Israel; whose goings forth have been of old, from everlasting. Therefore will he give them up, until the time that she which travaileth hath brought forth: then the remnant of his brethren shall return unto the children of Israel (Micah 5:2, 3).

Travailing in birth is a figure used in Israel:

> Before she travailed, she brought forth: before her pain came, she was delivered of a man child. Who hath heard such a thing? who hath seen such things? Shall the earth be made to bring forth in one day? or shall a nation be born at once? for as soon as Zion travailed, she brought forth her children (Isa. 66:7,8).

Being tormented reveals the extreme suffering that has come to Israel and will come because of satanic anti-Semitism.

b. The Red **DRAGON**—Satan (the second sign), verses 3, 4

Verses 3,4—And there appeared another wonder in heaven; and behold a great red dragon, having seven heads and ten horns, and seven crowns upon his heads. And his tail drew the third part of the stars of heaven, and did

cast them to the earth: and the dragon stood before the woman which was ready to be delivered, for to devour her child as soon as it was born.

And there was seen another sign in heaven, and behold, a great red dragon having seven heads and ten horns and on his head seven diadems (kingly crowns). And his tail draweth the third of the stars of heaven, and he did cast [aorist tense] them into the earth. And the dragon stood before the woman about to be delivered, that when she was delivered he might devour her child.

In this second sign the true character of Satan is revealed with all the wrappings removed.

(1) He is *great* because of his vast power (see Matt. 4:8, 9 where Satan offered the kingdoms of the world to Christ, for Satan controlled Rome which ruled the world).

(2) He is *red* because of the fact that he was a murderer from the beginning (John 8:44), he has no regard for human life.

(3) He is a *dragon* because of the viciousness of his character. He was originally created Lucifer, son of the morning (see Ezek. 28:12-19). He is now the epitome of evil and the depth of degredation.

The reason that the beast in chapter 13 is similar to the dragon is because both the restored Roman Empire and Antichrist are empowered and controlled by Satan. Rome, through the instrumentality of both Herod and Pilate, sought to destroy the child of the woman.

Seven heads suggest the perfection of wisdom which characterized the creation of Satan who was originally the "covering cherub." Of Satan Ezekiel writes:

Son of man, take up a lamentation upon the king of Tyrus, and say unto him, Thus saith the Lord GOD; Thou sealest up the sum, full of wisdom, and perfect in beauty (Ezek. 28:12).

Ten horns suggest the final division of the Roman Empire which is dominated by Satan and which is his final effort to rule this world. The crowns are on the horns, not on the heads, since it is delegated power—from Satan. The crowns represent kingly authority and rulership.

A third part of the stars of heaven indicates the vast extent of the rebellion in heaven when one third of the angelic host followed Satan to their own destruction. Daniel makes reference to this in an admittedly difficult passage (see Daniel 8:10 and Jude 5).

The dragon hates this child because it was predicted from the beginning that the child would be the undoing of Satan.

And I will put enmity between thee and the woman, and between thy seed and her seed; it shall bruise thy head, and thou shalt bruise his heel (Gen. 3:15).

c. The **CHILD** of the Woman—Jesus Christ, verses 5, 6

Verses 5, 6—And she brought forth a man child, who was to rule all nations with a rod of iron: and her child was caught up unto God, and to his throne. And the woman fled into the wilderness, where she hath a place prepared of God, that they should feed her there a thousand two hundred and threescore days.

3

And she was delivered of a son, a man child, who is to shepherd (rule) all the nations with a rod of iron, and her child was caught up unto God and His throne. And the woman fled into the wilderness, where she hath a place prepared of (from) God, that there they may nourish her a thousand two hundred and sixty (1260) days.

The *child* is Christ. He is easily identified here. I trust no one will fall into the error of equating the child with the church, as so many have done.

Who is to shepherd (rule) all the nations with a rod of iron is a clear-cut reference to Christ.

Thou shalt break them with a rod of iron; thou shalt dash them in pieces like a potter's vessel (Psa. 2:9).

For of a truth against thy holy child Jesus, whom thou hast anointed, both Herod, and Pontius Pilate, with the Gentiles, and the people of Israel, were gathered together, for to do whatsoever thy hand and thy counsel determined before to be done (Acts 4:27, 28).

Here Scripture interprets Scripture. The persecuted Christians are quoting the Second Psalm and identifying the One to rule with a rod of iron as the Lord Jesus Christ.

And her child was caught up unto God and His throne is a reference to the ascension of Christ.

And when he had spoken these things, while they beheld, he was taken up; and a cloud received him out of their sight. And while they looked stedfastly toward heaven as he went up, behold, two men stood by them in white apparel: which also said, Ye men of Galilee, why stand ye gazing up into heaven? this same Jesus, which is taken up from you into heaven, shall so come in like manner as ye have seen him go into heaven (Acts 1:9-11).

Looking unto Jesus the author and finisher of our faith; who for the joy that was set before him endured the cross, despising the shame, and is set down at the right hand of the throne of God (Heb. 12:2).

Remember that this book is the unveiling of the ascended Christ. The book of the Revelation rests upon the fact of the ascension. Christ is the one who has been opening the seals.

She brought forth a man child settles the identity of the woman. Israel is clearly the one from whom Christ came: "Who are Israelites . . . whom as concerning the flesh Christ came" (Rom. 9:4, 5).

But when the fulness of the time was come, God sent forth his Son, made of a woman, made under the law, to redeem them that were under the law, that we might receive the adoption of sons (Gal. 4:4, 5).

Now to Abraham and his seed were the promises made. He saith not, And to seeds, as of many; but as of one, And to thy seed, which is Christ (Gal. 3:16).

For unto us a child is born, unto us a son is given: and the government shall be upon his shoulder: and his name shall be called Wonderful, Counsellor, The mighty God, The everlasting Father, The Prince

4

of Peace. Of the increase of his government and peace there shall be no end, upon the throne of David, and upon his kingdom, to order it, and to establish it with judgment and with justice from henceforth even for ever. The zeal of the LORD of hosts will perform this (Isa. 9:6, 7).

Israel is persecuted by Satan and the particular period is identified as the last half of the Great Tribulation by the time period of 1260 days.

The wilderness where God preserves Israel may not be identified on the map, yet it is a literal wilderness. God protected and preserved Israel in the wilderness for 40 years when He led them out of Egypt. Could this be the same wilderness? We know that they are to leave Palestine; they will flee because of the abomination of desolation:

> Then let them which be in Judea flee into the mountains: let him which is on the housetop not come down to take any thing out of his house: neither let him which is in the field return back to take his clothes. And woe unto them that are with child, and to them that give suck in those days! But pray ye that your flight be not in the winter, neither on the sabbath day (Matt. 24:16-20).

Elijah retreated to the wilderness in the days of Ahab and Jezebel (see I Kings 19). At the arrest of John the Baptist, Jesus departed into the wilderness. While the exact geographical location is not pinpointed, it is prepared of God and Israel will be miraculously preserved there during the last half of the Great Tribulation.

d. MICHAEL, the Archangel, Wars with the Dragon, verses 7-12

Verses 7-9—And there was war in heaven: Michael and his angels fought against the dragon; and the dragon fought and his angels, and prevailed not; neither was their place found any more in heaven. And the great dragon was cast out, that old serpent, called the Devil, and Satan, which deceiveth the whole world: he was cast out into the earth, and his angels were cast out with him.

And there arose war in heaven, Michael and his angels going forth to war with the dragon. And the dragon warred and his angels, and they prevailed not, neither was their place found any more in heaven. And the great dragon was cast down, the old serpent, the one called (the) Devil, and the Satan, he that deceiveth the whole (inhabitated) world; he was cast down to the earth, and his angels with him were cast down.

This is a startling revelation—*war in heaven*. It is difficult to imagine there being war in heaven, but Satan still has access to heaven (see Job 1 and 2; Zech. 3:1-7; Luke 22:31), and he will not withdraw voluntarily. He must be thrown out.

Michael is the archangel (Jude 9). Evidently there are others (Dan. 10:13), but Michael has the peculiar ministry of the oversight of the nation Israel (Dan. 10:21; 12:1). Apparently Michael acts here in the interest of the nation Israel, as this takes place in the Great Tribulation.

Though the struggle was fierce, Michael and his angels prevailed and Satan and his angels are thrown out of heaven. Jesus referred to this:

5

And he said unto them, I beheld Satan as lightning fall from heaven (Luke 10:18).

There is no mistaking this creature, who is called the great dragon, for he is marked out with great detail. His fingerprints are put down here, because God knew that a great percentage of the preachers in this century would teach that he does not exist. If your enemy can get you to think he does not exist, he can get a good crack at you.

(1) *Old serpent* takes us back to the Garden of Eden. Our Lord said "he was a murderer from the beginning." The words "old" and "beginning" are akin, according to Vincent.

(2) *Devil* is a name which comes from the Greek *diabolos*, meaning "slanderer" or "accuser". He is so labeled in verse 10, "the accuser of our brethren." That is the reason that believers need an advocate:

My little children, these things write I unto you, that ye sin not. And if any man sin, we have an advocate with the Father, Jesus Christ the righteous (I John 2:1).

(3) *Satan* means "adversary." He is the awful adversary of God and of every one of God's children.

Be sober, be vigilant; because your adversary the devil, as a roaring lion, walketh about. seeking whom he may devour (I Pet. 5:8).

(4) *He that deceiveth the whole (inhabited) world.*

Satan deceives man relative to God and His Word (see Genesis 3:4).
Satan deceives man relative to man— he makes him out better than he is, yet he despises him (Gen. 3:5).
Satan deceives man relative to the world, the flesh and the devil (see temptation of Jesus in the synoptic gospels; also I John 2:15-17).
Satan deceives the world relative to the gospel—he does not mind man going to church, or even joining a dozen churches. but he does not want him to be saved: ". . . the god of this world hath blinded the minds of them which believe not, lest the light of the glorious gospel of Christ, who is the image of God, should shine unto them" (2 Cor. 4:4).

"Satan is to be dreaded as a lion;
More to be dreaded as a serpent;
And most to be dreaded as an angel."

Verses 10-12—And I heard a loud voice saying in heaven, Now is come salvation, and strength, and the kingdom of our God, and the power of his Christ: for the accuser of our brethren is cast down, which accused them before our God day and night. And they overcame him by the blood of the Lamb, and by the word of their testimony; and they loved not their lives unto the death. Therefore rejoice, ye heavens, and ye that dwell in them. Woe to the inhabiters of the earth and of the sea! for the devil is come down unto you, having great wrath, because he knoweth that he hath but a short time.

And I heard a great voice in heaven, saying, Now is come the salvation, and the power, and the kingdom of our God, and the authority [exousia] of His Christ; for the accuser of our brethren is cast down, the one accusing them be-

6

fore our God day and night. And they overcame him because of the blood of the Lamb, and because of the word of their testimony; and they loved not their life even unto death. Therefore, rejoice, O heavens, and ye that dwell in them. Woe for the earth and for the sea; because the devil is gone down unto you, having great wrath, knowing that he has but a short time.

And I heard reminds us that John is still the spectator and auditor of these events.

A great voice in heaven seems to refer to the Old Testament saints or the tribulation saints who have been martyred up to this point (see 6:9, 10), for they mention their brethren on the earth.

For the accuser of our brethren is cast down. There is finality in the tense of the verb. It means once and for all.

The first great demonstration of power exerted against evil, after the death and resurrection of Christ, is the casting out of Satan from heaven. When Christ died on the cross He paved the way for Satan being cast out of heaven:

> Blotting out the handwriting of ordinances that was against us, which was contrary to us, and took it out of the way, nailing it to his cross; and having spoiled principalities and powers, he made a show of them openly, triumphing over them in it (Col. 2:14,15).

This opens the way for the coming of four great blood-bought heavenly freedoms:

(1) *the salvation* (the person of Christ—His visible return to earth);
(2) *the power*
(3) *and the kingdom of our God,* revealing that the kingdom was not established at the first coming of Christ;
(4) *the authority of His Christ,* showing that Christ has not as yet taken over the governmental authority of this world.

The one accusing them day and night before our God reveals that this is part of the present strategy of Satan which attempts to thwart Christ's purposes with His Church today and the Tribulation saints tomorrow. This necessitates Christ's present ministry as advocate (see I John 2:1).

Victory for the accused saints comes through three avenues:

(1) *The blood of the Lamb,* revealing "the wonder working power of the blood of the Lamb." The many references to the blood of the Lamb necessitate it being there on display. This is not a crude conception—rather the crudity is in our sins.

> But if we walk in the light, as he is in the light, we have fellowship one with another, and the blood of Jesus Christ his Son cleanseth us from all sin (I John 1:7).

(2) *The word of their testimony.* revealing that they were true martyrs (witnesses). Those who are Christ's cannot deny Him.

> But whosoever shall deny me before men, him will I also deny before my Father which is in heaven (Matt. 10:33).

(3) *They loved not their life even unto death* is translated by Alford, "they carried their not-love of their life even unto death." which means they loved the Lord Jesus more than their own lives. Love of Christ is the real test of service:

7

He saith unto him the third time, Simon, son of Jonas, lovest thou me? Peter was grieved because he said unto him the third time, Lovest thou me? And he said unto him, Lord, thou knowest all things; thou knowest that I love thee. Jesus said unto him, Feed my sheep (John 21:17).

There are two radical views of the casting out of Satan from heaven. There is (1) rejoicing in heaven, for this awesome, treacherous, dangerous, and deadly serpent is out forever; and (2) there is woe on the earth. This is the third Woe which extends through the pouring out of the Seven Bowls of Wrath. The only consolation for the earth is that Satan's sojourn on earth is brief—42 months. It is an intensification of tribulation during this period.

e. The Dragon Persecutes the Woman, verses 13-16

Verses 13, 14—And when the dragon saw that he was cast unto the earth, he persecuted the woman which brought forth the man child. And to the woman were given two wings of a great eagle, that she might fly into the wilderness, into her place, where she is nourished for a time, and times, and half a time, from the face of the serpent.

This is the last wave of anti-Semitism to roll over the world, and it is the worst—because Satan is cast down to the earth and his time is short. Satan hates the nation Israel because Christ came from that nation according to the flesh (see Romans 9:5). This is "the time of Jacob's trouble." I cannot rejoice today to see the Jewish people returning to Palestine, for they are going back to the Great Tribulation. Our responsibility is to get the gospel to them so that they may be spared the horrors of the Great Tribulation.

The two wings of the great eagle is reminiscent of the grace of God in delivering Israel, in the past, from Egypt. God had said to them, "Ye have seen what I did to the Egyptians, how I bare you on eagles' wings, and brought you to myself" (Ex. 19:4). They had not come out by their own effort, or by their own ability. They came out because God brought them out—and eagles' wings became a symbol to them. Here again, in the Great Tribulation, Israel cannot deliver themselves, and no one is interested in delivering them, but God will get them out on eagles' wings—by His grace. (See author's booklet, *On Eagles' Wings*.)

Into the wilderness, unto her place has been variously identified; e.g. Petra, or the wilderness of the peoples of the world. Since Christ said, "Flee unto the mountains," we believe it to be a literal wilderness—possibly the same one in which Israel spent 40 years under Moses. This time it will be 42 months, for that is the meaning of *time, times and one half a time* (see 11:2). The important thing is not the place but the fact that God will protect them by His grace.

Where she is nourished reminds us that in the past God sustained them with manna from heaven and water from the rock. He will nourish them again in possibly the same way.

Verses 15, 16—And the serpent cast out of his mouth water as a flood after the woman, that he might cause her to be carried away of the flood. And the earth helped the woman, and the earth opened her mouth, and swallowed up the flood which the dragon cast out of his mouth.

And the serpent cast out of his mouth after the woman water as a river, that he might cause her to be carried away by the stream. And the earth helped the

8

woman, and the earth opened her mouth and swallowed up the river which the dragon cast out of his mouth.

In view of the fact that the wilderness is literal, the water also could be literal. God had delivered Israel out of the water, both at the beginning of the wilderness march (the Red Sea), and at the end of the wilderness march (the Jordan River). However, the floods of water could be armies flowing like a river upon them. This figure of speech has been adopted in the past (see Isaiah 8:7, 8).

In Ezekiel's picture of the last days, the king of the north is seen marching on Israel. How will he be stopped? No nation is there to stop him. But God is there and He will destroy him with natural forces when he invades Palestine.

And I will plead against him with pestilence and with blood; and I will rain upon him, and upon his bands, and upon the many people that are with him, an overflowing rain, and great hailstones, fire, and brimstone (Ezek. 38:22).

f. The **Remnant** of Israel, verse 17

Verse 17—And the dragon was wroth with the woman, and went to make war with the remnant of her seed, which keep the commandments of God, and have the testimony of Jesus Christ.

And the dragon was wroth with the woman, and he went away to make war with the rest of her seed, that keep the commandments of God and hold the testimony of Jesus.

The rest of her seed refers to the remnant who is God's witness in this period —the 144,000 who have been sealed. They are evidently witnessing throughout the world. These keep the commandments of God, which places them back under the law.

(This precludes the possibility of the witnesses being the Church.)

All anti-Semitism is Satan inspired, and will finally culminate in Satan making a supreme effort to destroy this nation. From the brick yards of Pharaoh's Egypt, Haman's gallows and Herod's cruel edict, to the world of the Great Tribulation, Satan has led the attack against these people because of the man-child —Jesus Christ.

Chapter 13

THEME: The two beasts—Beast out of the Sea and Beast out of the Earth.

OUTLINE:

g. **Wild Beast Out of the Sea—a Political Power and a Person, verses 1-10**
   (1). Wild Beast, **Description,** verses 1, 2
   (2). Wild Beast, **Death Dealing Stroke,** verse 3
   (3). Wild Beast, **Deity Assumed,** verses 4, 5
   (4). Wild Beast, **Defying God,** verses 6-8
   (5). Wild Beast, **Defiance Denied to Anyone,** verses 9, 10

h. **Wild Beast Out of the Earth—a Religious Leader, verses 11-18**
   (1). Wild Beast, **Description,** verse 11
   (2). Wild Beast, **Delegated Authority,** verses 12-14
   (3). Wild Beast, **Delusion Perpetrated on the World,** verses 15-17
   (4). Wlid Beast, **Designation,** verse 18

REMARKS:

Five performers who play conspicious parts in the events of the Great Tribulation were brought before us in chapter 12:

1. The Woman (Israel)
2. The Red Dragon (Satan)
3. The Child of the Woman (Christ)
4. Michael (the Archangel)
5. The Remnant (the 144,000 Sealed of Israel)

The final two (2) performers are brought before us in this chapter. They are the beast out of the sea and the beast out of the earth. Both are presented as wild beasts. It is bad enough to be a beast, but to be a wild beast compounds the injury. There is much disagreement among reputable Bible expositors as to the identity of the beasts. Some consider the first beast to be a person, while others treat him as the last form of the Roman Empire. Some treat the second beast as the Man of Sin, while others consider him merely as the prophet, or "the John the Baptist" type for the first beast.

These difficulties arise because it is impossible to separate a king from his kingdom. A dictator must have a realm over which he rules, or he is no dictator. Though it is difficult to distinguish the two, it seems that the first beast is the Antichrist, the ruler over the restored Roman Empire. "The throne of the wild beast" (16:10) makes it clear that the first beast is a man.

After determining the identity of the first beast, it is not difficult to identify the second. He is a man, the false prophet, the religious leader who leads in the worship of the first beast.

There is another view being held today that Antichrist is a denial of the person of Christ—rather than an actual person: Antichrist is false doctrine—rather than a person to be revealed (see Pentecost, *Things to Come*, p. 337).

The explanation is found in the meaning of the preposition, *anti*. It has two usages: first, *over against*; and second, *instead of or in place of*. It has both meanings in Scripture.

John alone uses the word *anti-christ*, and that in his first two epistles. There it has the meaning, it seems, of opposition to Christ:

> Little children, it is the last time: and as ye have heard that anti-christ shall come, even now are there many anti-christs; whereby we know that it is the last time. Who is a liar but he that denieth that Jesus is the Christ? He is anti-christ, that denieth the Father and the Son (I John 2:18, 22).

> And every spirit that confesseth not that Jesus Christ is come in the flesh is not of God: and this is that spirit of anti-christ, whereof ye have heard that it should come; and even now already is in the world (I John 4:3).

> For many deceivers are entered into the world, who confess not that Jesus Christ is come in the flesh. This is a deceiver and an anti-christ (II John 7).

The first beast represents this characteristic.

The second characteristic is portrayed by the second beast. He is a false Christ; and our Lord warned of such in the Olivet Discourse;

> For there shall arise false Christs, and false prophets, and shall show great signs and wonders; insomuch that, if it were possible, they shall deceive the very elect (Matt. 24:24).

The entire system of the two beasts is anti-christ in its final form.

g. Wild Beast Out of the Sea—a Political Power and a Person, verses 1-10

(1). Wild Beast, DESCRIPTION, verses 1, 2

Verse 1—And I stood upon the sand of the sea, and saw a beast rise up out of the sea, having seven heads and ten horns, and upon his horns ten crowns, and upon his heads the name of blasphemy.

And he stood on the sand of the sea; and I saw a (wild) beast coming up out of the sea, having ten horns and seven heads, and on his horns ten diadems, and upon his heads names of blasphemy.

The dragon (Satan) stands on the sand of the sea, and it is he who brings the wild beast out of the sea and dominates it. This is his masterpiece. He is a person who heads up the old Roman Empire. God apparently steps aside and gives him full reign.

The sea is representative of the nations (Gentiles).

A wild beast is similar in description to the fourth beast (non-descript) in Daniel, chapter 7. There it represents the prophetic history of the Roman Empire down to the "little horn" and his destruction.

At the time of the writing of John, much of the prophecy of Daniel had been fulfilled. John was living in the time of the Roman Empire, having been exiled to the isle of Patmos by the Roman emperor, Domitian. Already signs of weakness and decay were visible in the empire. John was a spectator to that which was still future. The emphasis is upon the rule of the "little horn" of Daniel 7. The "little horn" is set before us as the wild beast, for he is now ruling and controlling the Roman Empire in this prophecy. The "little horn" and the wild beast are identical here. The wild beast is the Man of Sin and

Antichrist—the final world dictator. The last verse of this chapter confirms this view: "Let him that hath understanding count the number of *the beast:* for it *is* the number of a *man* (verse 18).

The ten horns with ten diadems speak of the ten-fold division of the Roman Empire in the time of the Great Tribulation. The horns are the ten kings who rule over this ten-fold division of the Roman Empire. This interpretation is confirmed by 17:12. At the present writing we are seeing straws in the wind, and we wonder if these movements are the beginning of the ten-nation kingdom. The following are excerpts from current news periodicals:

> Christian Herter, the former Secretary of State, said further that Treaty of Rome which became effective Jan. 1, 1958, created the following institutions: first, a commission which proposes community policy and has day to day administrative authority. This commission is composed of nine men. Second, a council of ministers which decide community policy and it has prime executive responsibility. This council of ministers is made up of representatives of the six member states. Third, an assembly, which serves as a limited parliament. This assembly is a 142 man body appointed by the six member states. And fourth, it set up a court of justice which passes judgment on legal issues arising under the treaty. This court of justice is a seven man appointed body. Herter concludes his summary of that which was created in the Roman Treaty by saying, "The importance of all these institutions is more than administrative. They represent the nucleus from which a European government could evolve."

> . . . this international trading area embracing six nations of France, West Germany, Italy, the Netherlands, Belgium and Luxembourg, in a single economic union and serving 170,000,000 European customers, is proving an economic success beyond all the expectations of its founders. The British government, in a revolutionary decision last fall, made application to join the six countries, although this would cause Britain to alter her ties with the commonwealth, abandon her historic aloofness from the continent and to lose some of her own sovereignty. Norway, Denmark and Ireland are almost certain to follow suit. This will create a European economic federation of *ten nations* and 250,000,000 people whose goods, farm products and workers will soon be able to move as freely across national frontiers as ours move across state boundaries in the United States.

The "little horn" comes to power by first putting down three, afterward he dominates all and becomes the world dictator (see author's book, *Delving Through Daniel*, chapter 7).

The seven heads are not so easily identified. They are interpreted in chapter 17: 9, 10 as seven kings. These do not reign contemporaneously as the ten horns do, but they appear in a chronological order. (a) Some have interpreted them as representing certain Roman emperors, as Domitian who was then ruling (compare Govett and Newell). (b) Others interpret these seven heads as the forms of government through which the Roman Empire passed: kings, consuls, dictators, decemvirs, military tribunes, and emperors (compare Scott and Pentecost). (c) A third view is that the seven heads could represent seven great nations of antiquity which blasphemed God: Rome, Greece, Media-Persia, Chaldea, Egypt, and Assyria. The kingdom of the Beast would be the seventh, which is yet to come (compare Seiss). (d) Another likely view is that the seven heads correspond to the seven heads of the dragon, which denote exceptional wisdom. Satan energizes the Man of Sin, the last dictator. (See verse 3 for the interpretation of the horns which we consider more adequate.)

All seven heads are guilty of blasphemy. Blasphemy manifests itself in two ways, according to Govett, (a) making oneself equal with God, usurping His place; (b) slandering and taking God's name in vain. The emperors of Rome were guilty of the first form: the Pharisees were guilty of the latter—when they blasphemed the Holy Spirit (see Mark 3:29). The Beast is guilty of both forms, as we shall see in verse 5.

Verse 2—And the beast which I saw was like unto a leopard, and his feet were as the feet of a bear, and his mouth as the mouth of a lion; and the dragon gave him his power, and his seat, and great authority.

And the wild beast which I saw was like unto a panther, and his feet were as the feet of a bear, and his mouth as the mouth of a lion: and the dragon gave him his power, and his throne, and great authority.

John reminds us that he is still a spectator to this beast.

John notes that he is a composite beast. He combines the characteristics of the other beasts which Daniel saw in his vision in Daniel 7:

(a) The outward appearance was like unto a panther (leopard).

After this I beheld, and lo another, like a leopard, which had upon the back of it four wings of a fowl; the beast had also four heads; and dominion was given to it (Dan. 7:6).

This was Greece. Greece was noted for its brilliance and advancement in the arts and sciences. The empire of the Beast will have all the outward culture which was the glory of Greece.

(b) *Feet of a bear* reminds us of the second beast of Daniel.

And behold another beast, a second, like to a bear, and it raised up itself on one side, and it had three ribs in the mouth of it between the teeth of it: and they said thus unto it, Arise, devour much flesh (Dan. 7:5).

This was Media-Persia, noted for its pagan splendor, as it padded and waddled over the earth like a Gargantua.

(c) *Mouth of a lion* reminds us of the first beast of Daniel 7—the lion:

The first was like a lion, and had eagle's wings: I beheld till the wings thereof were plucked, and it was lifted up from the earth, and made stand upon the feet as a man, and a man's heart was given to it (Dan. 7:4).

This was Babylonian autocracy. When Nebuchadnezzar ordered death for his wise men, and the fiery furnace for the three Hebrew children, there was none to question his authority. He was the "head of gold."

Though the Man of Sin will be one of the toes, composed partly of clay, he will rule with the autocracy and dictatorial authority of Nebuchadnezzar. This final world dictator comes to its zenith under the domination of the Beast.

The source of his power is found in Satan, who raises him up, empowers and energizes him for the dastardly dictatorial job. He is the closest to an incarnation of Satan that appears in Scripture. Remember that Luke said that Satan had entered into Judas Iscariot (see Luke 22:3). Also, Christ used similar language with Simon Peter (see Matt. 16:23). Is the Man of Sin the incarnation of Satan? (See II Thess. 2:9.)

(2). Wild Beast, **DEATH DEALING** Stroke, verse 3

Verse 3—And I saw one of his heads as it were wounded to death; and his deadly wound was healed: and all the world wondered after the beast.

And one of his heads as though it had been slain unto death; and his stroke of death was healed; and the whole (inhabited) earth wondered after the beast.

(a) This verse, together with Revelation 17:8, has led many to the view that Satan actually raises the Beast from the dead (compare Seiss, Govett, and Newell). The Beast is interpreted here as a man. That the early church, for the most part, held to this view is indisputable. They disagreed as to the identity of the Beast. Some thought he was Judas Iscariot. Others identified him as Nero. Even Augustine, in his day, wrote: "What means the declaration, that the mystery of iniquity doth already work? Some suppose it to be spoken of the Roman Emperor, and therefore Paul did not speak in plain words, although he always expected that what he said would be understood as applying to Nero, whose doings already appeared like those of Antichrist. Hence it was that some suspected that he would rise from the dead as Antichrist."[1]

(b) Others take the view that the Beast here refers to the Roman Empire, over which the Beast rules. The Imperial form of government, under which Rome fell, will be restored in a startling manner. This is the head wounded unto death and restored to life, according to this view (Scofield and Ironside). The Roman Empire has not truly died, for it fell apart and lives on in the fragments of the nations of Western Europe today. Rome is waiting for some personality who is capable of putting the empire back together. This man is the Beast. Rome is like Humpty Dumpty that sat on the wall and had a great fall. All the king's horses and all the king's men cannot put Humpty Dumpty together again—but Antichrist can and will.

Both of these views have much to commend them, while both have serious objections. There can be no real resurrection of an evil man before the Great White Throne judgment. Only Christ can raise the dead of both saved and lost, and Christ will raise the dead who stand before the Great White Throne (Rev. 20:11-15).

> Marvel not at this: for the hour is coming, in the which all that are in the graves shall hear his [Christ's] voice, and shall come forth; they that have done good, unto the resurrection of life; and they that have done evil, unto the resurrection of damnation (John 5:28, 29).

Satan has no power to raise the dead. He is not a life-giver; but he is a devil, a destroyer and a death-dealer.

The Roman Empire is to be revitalized and made to cohere in a miraculous manner under the world dictator, the Beast—yet verse 3 seems to demand a more adequate explanation than this.

(c) I believe that the Beast is a *man* who will exhibit a counterfeit and imitation resurrection. This will be the great delusion, the big lie of the Great Tribulation period.

[1] Seiss, *The Apocalypse*, p. 398 footnote.

14

His stroke of death was healed shows the blasphemous imitation of the death and resurrection of Christ. The challenge will be, "What has Christ done that Antichrist has not not done?" The faithful will say, "Christ rose from the dead." Their boast will be, "So did Antichrist!" The Roman Empire will spring back into existence under the cruel hand of a man who faked a resurrection; and a gullible world that rejected Christ is finally taken in by this forgery.

And then shall that Wicked be revealed, whom the Lord shall consume with the spirit of his mouth, and shall destroy with the brightness of his coming: even him, whose coming is after the working of Satan with all power and signs and lying wonders. And with all deceivableness of unrighteousness in them that perish; because they received not the love of the truth, that they might be saved. And for this cause God shall send them strong delusion, that they should believe a lie: that they all might be damned who believe not the truth, but had pleasure in unrighteousness (II Thes. 2:8-12).

(3). Wild Beast, **DEITY ASSUMED**, verses 4, 5

Verse 4—And they worshipped the dragon which gave power unto the beast: and they worshipped the beast, saying, Who is like unto the beast? who is able to make war with him?

And they worshipped the dragon, because he gave his authority unto the beast; and they worshipped the beast, saying, who is like unto the beast? and who is able to war with him?

This is the supreme moment for Satan, as he has directed all of his energies toward this goal. He is not opposed to religion, as most folk believe, but he is the founder and promoter of it—only it is his intense desire to be the object of worship. For a brief moment the world will worship him, because the world will be worshipping the Beast. The whole world will be helpless and in slavery to the Beast. There will be no opposition to him.

Who is like unto the beast is, as Vincent comments, an awful parody on the worship of the true God (see Isa. 40:25; Psa. 113:5; Micah 7:18). All through the Word of God it is said that God has no equal. That is one reason it is so difficult for us to comprehend God—we have no measuring stick to measure Him. To whom can we compare Him? Who is like Him? No one. Yet that which is said of God will be said of the Beast. Worship of the Beast is the deadly blasphemy of the last half of the Great Tribulation (see II Thes. 2:3, 4; Daniel 7:25; 8:10-12; 9:27; 11:31, 36; Matt. 24:24). The religions of the world are marching toward the dark day of total devil worship.

Verse 5—And there was given unto him a mouth speaking great things and blasphemies; and power was given unto him to continue forty and two months.

And there was given to him a mouth speaking great things and blasphemies; and there was given to him authority to continue (to work) forty and two months.

And there was given to him occurs two times in this verse, and four times in the remainder of this chapter—six in all. Under the permissive will of God the cup of iniquity, by Satan working through the Beast, will be filled to the brim. Evil must have its day—this period gives it its day. (See the last list of Scripture references under verse 4, which reveal also the big mouth of the Beast speaking blasphemies.)

The period of *forty and two months* refers to the last half of the Great Tribulation. The literal meaning is *to work during forty and two months.*

(4). Wild Beast, **DEFYING GOD,** verses 6-8

Verse 6—And he opened his mouth in blasphemy against God, to blaspheme his name, and his tabernacle, and them that dwell in heaven.

And he opend his mouth for blasphemies against God, to blaspheme His name and His tabernacle which dwell (tabernacle) in heaven.

This is the dreadful limit to which the Beast goes in blasphemy. It is against Christ and His Church in heaven.

Verses 7, 8—And it was given unto him to make war with the saints, and to overcome them: and power was given him over all kindreds, and tongues, and nations. And all that dwell upon the earth shall worship him, whose names are not written in the book of life of the Lamb slain from the foundation of the world.

And it was given unto him to make war with the saints and to overcome them: and there was given to him authority over every tribe and people and tongue and nation. And all that dwell on the earth shall worship him, every one whose name hath not been written from the foundation of the world in the book of life of the Lamb that hath been slain.

He blasphemed Christ and the Church in heaven which he could not touch, but he made war with the saints on earth. Over them he gained a temporary victory. This is the darkest hour in the history of the world. The Beast is a world dictator. The whole world worships him—with the exception of those whose names are written in the Lamb's book of life. This again is the perseverance of the saints. They will hold out to the end, because they are in the nail-pierced hands of Christ.

But he that shall endure unto the end, the same shall be saved (Matt. 24:13).

(5). Wild Beast, **DEFIANCE DENIED TO ANYONE,** verses 9, 10

Verses 9, 10—If any man have an ear, let him hear. He that leadeth into captivity shall go into captivity: he that killeth with the sword must be killed with the sword. Here is the patience and the faith of the saints.

If any man hath an ear, let him hear. If any one is for captivity (bring together captives) into captivity he goeth (away): if any man shall kill with the sword, with the sword must he be killed. Here is the patience and the faith of the saints.

If any man is a thrice repeated invitation to the ear of any one who will hear the word of God at any time, in any age. "Faith cometh by hearing, and hearing by the word of God."

This verse contains a warning to anyone who dares to fight against the Beast with physical force. This is the Dragon's day, and the Beast's hour. God is letting him go the limit. Satan will not be able to say from the pit of hell through the eternal ages, "God never gave me a chance." God is warning His own not to resist him either.

Patience, which means suffering and faith, are the passwords of the day for God's saints in this hour of earth's travail and hell's holiday.

h. **The Wild Beast Out of the Earth—a Religious Leader, verses 11-18**

(1) Wild Beast—**DESCRIPTION,** verse 11

16

Verse 11—And I beheld another beast coming up out of the earth and he had two horns like a lamb, and he spake as a dragon.

And I saw another wild beast coming up out of the earth and he had two horns like a lamb, and he was speaking as a dragon.

This wild Beast is easier to identify than was the first. The first Beast comes out of the sea, which is symbolic of the nations and peoples of the world (see Daniel 7:2, 3; Matt. 13:47). The earth from which this second Beast arises is symbolic of Palestine. It is naturally assumed that the second Beast comes from Israel.

And he had two horns like a lamb suggests that he is an imitation of Christ, "the Lamb of God that taketh away the sin of the world." This pseudo-lamb does not subtract sin but adds and multiplies it. He does not come to do his own will but the will of the first Beast. He is a counterfeit Christ. He will do a lot of talking about loving everyone, but underneath he is a dangerous beast.

And he was speaking as a dragon reveals his true character and that he is an instrument of Satan. He is the false prophet (Revelation 16:13; 19:20; 20:10). Our Lord warned specifically of this one, as well as those who go before him:

> Beware of false prophets, which come to you in sheep's clothing, but inwardly they are ravening wolves (Matt. 7:15).

> For there shall arise false Christs, and false prophets, and shall shew great signs and wonders; insomuch that, if it were possible, they shall deceive the very elect (Matt. 24:24).

The false prophet is the "John the Baptist" to the first Beast. Some have identified him as King Saul or Judas. This is a mere assumption.

(2). Wild Beast—DELEGATED Authority, verses 12-14

Verse 12—And he exerciseth all the power of the first beast before him, and causeth the earth and them which dwell therein to worship the first beast, whose deadly wound was healed.

And he exerciseth all the authority of the first wild beast in his presence. And he maketh the earth and the dwellers therein to worship the first wild beast, whose wound of death was healed.

He has a delegated authority from the first wild Beast which makes him subservient to the first wild Beast.

He obviously leads in a movement to exterminate the harlot of Revelation 17 and the last vestige of an apostate church with its humanism (see Revelation 17: 16, 17). Then the false prophet will offer the world something new to worship— the first wild Beast, the wilful king, the Man of Sin, the last world dictator (see Daniel 11:36-39; Matt. 24:24; IIThes. 2:3-10).

Whose wound of death was healed shows that both the first and second Beasts are faith healers and miracle workers. This is the big lie and "strong delusion" (see verse 3).

Verses 13, 14—And he doeth great wonders so that he maketh fire come down from heaven on the earth in the sight of men, and deceiveth them that dwell on the earth by the means of those miracles which he had power to do in the sight of the beast; saying to them that dwell on the earth, that they

should make an image to the beast, which had the wound by a sword, and did live.

And he doeth great signs, that he should even make fire to come down out of heaven into the earth in the sight of men. And he deceiveth the dwellers on the earth through (dia) the signs which it was given him to do in the presence of the wild beast; saying to the dwellers on the earth that they should make an image (eikon) to the beast who hath the stroke of the sword and lived.

The false prophet is a worker of signs and miracles (see again Matt. 24:24). Our Lord warned against this false prophet. His deception is that he apes Elijah in bringing fire down from heaven. He is a combination of Jannes and Jambres:

> Then Pharaoh also called the wise men and the sorcerers: now the magicians of Egypt, they also did in like manner with their enchantments. For they cast down every man his rod, and they became serpents: but Aaron's rod swallowed up their rods (Ex. 7:11, 12).

John the Baptist specifically said that he himself had nothing to do with fire:

> I indeed baptize you with water unto repentance: but he that cometh after me is mightier than I, whose shoes I am not worthy to bear: he shall baptize you with the Holy Ghost, and with fire (Matt. 3:11).

The false prophet plays with fire until he is cast into the lake of fire (see Revelation 19:20). The world is taken in by this deception—with the exception of the elect. They cannot be deceived.

The false prophet shows his hand by causing to be made an image of the Man of Sin. The word for image is *eikon* which means likeness. The big production is a likeness that emphasizes the wound of death that was healed. It is interesting to note that the Lord Jesus did not permit anything connected with His physical appearance to survive. But the likeness of the Antichrist will evidently be placed in the temple at Jerusalem and is the "abomination of desolation" to which our Lord referred:

> When ye therefore shall see the abomination of desolation, spoken of by Daniel the prophet, stand in the holy place, (whoso readeth, let him understand:) (Matt 25:15).

See also Daniel 12:11; 11:31; 9:27; Matt. 24:16-21; Ex. 20:4-6. The appearance of this image ushers in the darkest hour of the Great Tribulation, as the remainder of this chapter reveals. Is not this what Paul is referring to in II Thes. 2:4?

(3). Wild Beast, **DELUSION** Perpetrated on the World, verses 15-17

Verses 15-17—And he had power to give life unto the image of the beast, that the image of the beast should both speak, and cause that as many as would not worship the image of the beast should be killed. And he caused all, both small and great, rich and poor, free and bond, to receive a mark in their right hand, or in their foreheads: And that no man might buy or sell, save he that had the mark, or the name of the beast, or the number of his name.

And it was given to him to give breath (pneuma) to the image of the wild beast, that the image of the wild beast should both speak, and cause that as many as should not worship the image of the wild beast should be killed. And he causeth all, the small and the great, and the rich and the poor, and the free

18

and the slave, that there be given them a mark on their right hand or upon their forehead; and that no one should be able to buy or to sell, except the one having the mark, even the name of the beast or the number of his name.

And it was given to him to give breath to the image of the wild beast is some clever deception used to enhance the strong delusion that the world, with the exception of the elect, might believe a lie. (Read again II Thes. 2:9, 10). This second Beast is directing all worship to the first Beast. He fulfills the role of a John the Baptist, "He (the first Beast) must increase."

He will achieve the goal of present day religionists: one religion for the whole world. Have you noticed today the tremendous move to bring together the religions of the world? A startling comment comes from a Jewish rabbi:

"Whether Messiah is a person or an assembly is of minor importance," said Chief Rabbi Marcus Melchoir of Denmark. "I believe Messianic times would come if the United Nations were made Messiah."

If this rabbi would be willing to accept the U. N. as Messiah, do you think he would not recognize as Messiah a man who is able to do what the U. N. apparently cannot do—put Europe back together and bring about world peace? The frightful alternative for refusing to worship the Beast is the sentence of death. The world has no choice.

He weds religion and business. The philosophy of the world is, "a man must eat to live." No one will be able to buy or sell who does not have the mark of the Beast. There will be no exception to this. No class is beyond this order. This is world dictatorship with a vengeance.

What is the mark of the Beast? In John's day soldiers were branded by their commanders, slaves by their masters, and those attached to certain pagan temples were branded by the mark of the god or goddess. Ptolemy Philopator had all Jews in Alexandria marked with the ivy leaf, symbol of Dionysus. In our day a newspaper columnist who wrote an article entitled. "Living by the Numbers," deplored the fact that we have to carry so many different cards in our wallets and concluded with this paragraph:

It would simplify matters if the government would assign each of us a single, all-purpose number which we could have tatooed across the forehead to spare us the trouble of carrying all those cards.

But what is the mark of the Beast? It is not given us to know. Any explanation is gratuitous assumption. We trust that no one who reads these pages will find it necessary to know.

(4). Wild Beast, **DESIGNATION,** verse 18

Verse 18—Here is wisdom. Let him that hath understanding count the number of the beast: for it is the number of a man; and his number is Six hundred three score and six.

Here is wisdom. He that hath understanding, let him count the number of the beast; for it is the number of man; and his number is six hundred and sixty and six.

Here is wisdom seems to be rather an ironical declaration when we consider

19

the maze of speculation accumulated through the centuries on this verse. However, the meaning is that the problem of the numbers here is extremely difficult. The welter of speculation is proof of this.

Suffice it to say that six is the number of man—just short of seven, the number of completion. It is repeated here three times.

In the Greek there is a very beautiful arrangement of this number:

hexakosioi	—	600
hexekonta	—	60
hex	—	6

A numerical value is attached to each lettter. We must let it stand there, for the visible number of the Beast and its meaning awaits the day of his manifestation.

It is not for us to be anxious to know the number of the Beast, rather that we might know Him (Christ).

> That I might know him, and the power of his resurrection, and the fellowship of his sufferings, being made conformable unto his death; if by any means I might attain unto the resurrection of the dead. Not as though I had already attained, either were already perfect: but I follow after, if that I may apprehend that for which also I am apprehended of Christ Jesus. Brethren, I count not myself to have apprehended; but this one thing I do, forgetting those things which are behind, and reaching forth unto those things which are before, I press toward the mark for the prize of the high calling of God in Christ Jesus (Phil. 3:10-14).

The only positive and important item for us today is that the first Beast is a man. There is a lesson.

> Thus said the LORD; Cursed be the man that trusteth in man, and maketh flesh his arm, and whose heart departeth from the LORD. For he shall be like the heath in the desert, and shall not see when good cometh; but shall inhabit the parched places in the wilderness, in a salt land and not inhabited.

> Blessed is the man that trusteth in the LORD, and whose hope the LORD is. For he shall be as a tree planted by the waters, and that spreadeth out her roots by the river, and shall not see when heat cometh, but her leaf shall be green; and shall not be careful in the year of drought, neither shall cease from yielding fruit (Jer. 17:5-8).

Chapter 14

THEME: The Lamb on Mt. Zion, the everlasting gospel preached in the world, Babylon will fall, judgment and blessing announced, the coming of Armageddon.

OUTLINE:

4. **Looking to the End of the Great Tribulation,** Chapter 14

   a. **Picture** of the Lamb with the 144,000, verses 1-5
   b. **Proclamation** of the Everlasting Gospel, verses 6, 7
   c. **Pronouncement** of Judgment on Babylon, verse 8
   d. **Pronouncement** of Judgment on Those Who Received the Mark of the Beast, verses 9-12
   e. **Praise** for Those Who Die in the Lord, verse 13
   f. **Preview** of Armageddon, verses 14-20

REMARKS:

This chapter constitutes a haiatus in the series of seven performers. It is obvious that this interlude could not be fitted in between the sixth and seventh performers who are the two wild Beasts. They had to be considered together, as they are like Siamese twins and the continuity between them could not be broken.

Therefore, this interlude follows the seventh performer in recognition of the logical sequence of this book—which is not a hodgepodge of visions. But unfolds in a logical, chronological, and mathematical order.

Certain performers are called to our attention in this chapter to give a full orbed view of the spectacular events of the previous chapter. It is clear from chapter 13 that this is the darkest day and the most horrible hour in history. It is truly hell's holiday. Every thoughtful mind must inevitably ask the question, "How did God's people fare during this period? Could they make it through to the end with overwhelming odds against them?" The shepherd who began with 144,000 sheep is now identified with them as a Lamb with 144,000. He did not lose one, for He redeemed them. He will have the last word; Babylon will fall and the followers of the Beast will be judged. Many of His own became martyrs, but they did not lose—they won. Their works follow them. The Lamb is returning to the earth. The morning is coming, the darkness will fade away, and the Sun of righteousness will arise with healing in His wings.

COMMENT:

   a. **PICTURE** of the Lamb with the 144,000, verses 1-5

Verse 1—And I looked, and, lo, a Lamb stood on the mount Zion, and with him an hundred forty and four thousand, having his Father's name written on their foreheads.

And I saw, and behold, the Lamb standing on the Mt. Zion, and with Him a hundred and forty and four thousand, having His name, and the name of His Father, written on their foreheads.

21

And I saw indicates that John is still the spectator to these events. The reel continues to roll and the story continues to unfold.

The Lamb is the Lord Jesus Christ (see 5:6, 8, 12, 13; 6:1, 16; 7:9, 10, 14, 17; 12:11; 13:8).

Mt. Zion is at Jerusalem. Verse 1 pictures the placid and pastoral scene which opens the Millennial Kingdom.

Yet have I set my king upon my holy hill of Zion (Psa. 2:6).

The 144,000 we believe to be the ones sealed in chapter 7, although there are some problems connected with this view. They came through the Great Tribulation like the three Hebrew children came through the fiery furnace. Notice that the Lamb is standing with them on Mt. Zion. Although He is in His person the Lamb, He is also the Shepherd. He started out with 144,000 and when He has come through the Great Tribulation He has not 143,999 — He has 144,000. In this hour when the pressures of Satan bear us down, the living, victorious Christ is available to us.

They still have the seal upon their foreheads, which puts them in contrast to those who have the mark of the Beast.

Verses 2, 3—And I heard a voice from heaven, as the voice of many waters, and as the voice of a great thunder: and I heard the voice of harpers harping with their harps: and they sung as it were a new song before the throne, and before the four beasts, and the elders: and no man could learn that song but the hundred and forty and four thousand which were redeemed from the earth.

And I heard a voice from heaven, as the voice of many waters, and as the voice of a great thunder: and the voice which I heard (was) as (the voice) of harpers harping with their harps: and they sing as it were a new song before the throne, and before the four living creatures and the elders: and no man could learn the song save the hundred and forty and four thousand, even they that had been purchased out of the earth.

And I heard. John is not only a spectator but he is an auditor to this scene.

The 144,000 join the heavenly chorus in the Millennium. (Have you ever heard a choir of 144,000?) Up to this time earth has been out of tune with heaven (see 5:8-10), but here the rule of Satan is over and heaven and earth are in tune. The 144,000 learn the new song and join in the harmony of heaven. God has put His harpers in heaven, while the 144,000 are on earth on Mt. Zion.

Purchased out of the earth means that they have been purchased to enter the Millennium on earth, not taken to heaven. No one can sing this song but the redeemed; no one can sing praises unto God but the redeemed.

Heaven and earth are brought into marvelous harmony during the Millennium. What a contrast to chapter 13 where earth is in rebellion against heaven under the Beasts. Here all is tranquility under the Lamb.

Verses 4, 5—These are they which were not defiled with women; for they are virgins. These are they which follow the Lamb withersoever he goeth. These were redeemed from among men, being the firstfruits unto God and

to the Lamb. And in their mouth was found no guile; for they are without fault before the throne of God.

These are they that were not defiled (besmirched) with women; for they are virgins (parthenoi). These are they that follow the Lamb whithersoever He goeth. These were purchased from among men, to be the firstfruits unto God and unto the Lamb. And in their mouth was found no lie: they are without blemish.

Were not defiled with women; for they are virgins can have a literal or spiritual sense—or both. The period of the great tribulation is one of unparalleled suffering. The 144,000 have been through that period. The abnormal times demanded an abnormal state. Jeremiah lived at a critical time, and God forbade him to marry because of the dark days:

> The word of the LORD came also unto me, saying, Thou shalt not take thee a wife, neither shalt thou have sons or daughters in this place. For thus said the LORD concerning the sons and concerning the daughters that are born in this place, and concerning their mothers that bare them, and concerning their fathers that begat them in this land: They shall die of grievous deaths; they shall not be lamented; neither shall they be buried; but they shall be as dung upon the face of the earth: and they shall be consumed by the sword, and by famine; and their carcasses shall be meat for the fowls of heaven, and for the beasts of the earth (Jer. 16:1-4).

Our Lord pronounced a woe upon those who were with child during the Great Tribulation:

> And woe unto them that are with child, and to them that give suck in those days! (Matt 24:19.)

During the church age marriage is honorable and the bed undefiled (see I Cor. 7:1-9; 25-31). However, God's injunction to Noah to multiply and replenish the earth is hardly the Scripture to apply to a world faced with a population explosion and at a time when believers can see the approach of the end of the age.

During the Great Tribulation there will be an exaggerated emphasis upon sex and obviously immorality will prevail. The 144,000 will have kept themselves aloof from the sins of the Great Tribulation.

Considering adultery in a spiritual sense, idolatry was classified as spiritual fornication in the Old Testament. Ezekiel 16 is God's severe indictment against Israel for fornication and adultery—which was idolatry. The 144,000 have kept themselves from the worship of the Beast and his image during the Great Tribulation.

Firstfruits unto God and unto the Lamb has definite reference to Israel:

> For if the casting away of them be the reconciling of the world, what shall the receiving of them be, but life from the dead? For if the firstfruits be holy, the lump is also holy: and if the root be holy, so are the branches (Rom. 11:15, 16).

This 144,000 will evidently occupy a unique place in the millennial Kingdom. They evidently will be in the vanguard with the Lamb when He returns to set up the Kingdom (see 19:14).

In their mouth was found no lie simply means that they had not participated in the big lie of the Beast when he used "lying wonders."

They are without blemish because they are clothed with the righteousness of Christ.

b. PROCLAMATION of the Everlasting Gospel, verses 6, 7

Verses 6, 7—And I saw another angel fly in the midst of heaven, having the everlasting gospel to preach unto them that dwell on the earth, and to every nation, and kindred, and tongue, and people, saying with a loud voice, Fear God and give glory to him; for the hour of his judgment is come: and worship him that made heaven, and earth, and the sea, and the fountains of waters.

And I saw another angel flying in mid heaven, having an eternal gospel (good tidings) to proclaim unto (over) them that dwell (sit) on the earth, and unto (over) every nation and tribe and tongue and people; and he saith with a great voice, Fear God and give Him glory, for the hour of His judgment is come: and worship Him that made the heaven and the earth and sea and fountains of water.

Another angel denotes another radical change in protocol of God's communication with the earth. This angel is the first in a parade of six "another" angels (see verses 8, 9, 15, 17, 18).

During this age the Gospel has been committed to men, and they alone are the messengers (see I Pet. 1:12). At the beginning of the Great Tribulation men are the messengers of God, as the 144,000 reveal. Even the two witnesses, with supernatural power, did not stand up against Satan, but were removed from the satanic scene of earth. Angels, as well as men, were the messengers of the Old Testament—"the word spoken by angels was steadfast" (Heb. 2:2). The times are so intense in this period that only angels can get the messages of God through to the world. Angels are indestructible.

Flying in mid heaven is no longer a ridiculous statement to a generation that has been treated to flying saucers and satellites in orbit. At this writing (December, 1962) we have a satellite rotating the earth, Telstar, which has made worldwide television a practical reality.

This angel will be a broadcasting station in space to the entire world.

An eternal gospel reveals that it is not the gospel of grace, the message of today. The content of it confirms this. On the other hand, it is not judgment. It is eternal, for it is basic and goes back to the beginning. It is an acknowledgment of God. *Fear God* is the basic requirement—"The fear of the Lord is the beginning of wisdom" (Prov. 9:10). It is a recognition of God as creator. The present day spread of atheism will find its full fruition in the Great Tribulation. This is a final call to man back to that which is basic. Noah proclaimed a coming judgment and warned the world: no one accepted or believed him. Jonah warned a city, and the entire population turned to God.

c. PRONOUNCEMENT of Judgment on Babylon, verse 8

Verse 8—And there followed another angel, saying, Babylon is fallen, is fallen, that great city, because she made all nations drink of the wine of the wrath of her fornication.

And another angel, a second, followed saying, Fell, fell is Babylon the great, that hath made all the nations to drink of the wine of the wrath of her fornication.

A reading of Hyslop's book, *The Two Babylons*, reveals that Babylon has been Satan's headquarters from the beginning.

This second angel runs ahead and announces that which is yet to come as if it had already taken place, *fell, fell is Babylon*. This is, in the Greek, the prophetic aorist. In other words, God's prophetic Word is so sure that He speaks as though the event had already taken place.

Babylon will evidently be rebuilt during the Great Tribulation period (see the author's book, *Initiation Into Isaiah*, chap. 13).

The idolatry of Babylon is a divine intoxication which will fascinate the entire world:

Babylon hath been a golden cup in the LORD'S hand, that made all the earth drunken: the nations have drunken of her wine; therefore the nations are mad (Jer. 51:7).

And I will punish the world for their evil, and the wicked for their iniquity; and I will cause the arrogancy of the proud to cease, and will lay low the haughtiness of the terrible (Isa. 13:11).

This brings down the wrath of God upon the world (see Jer. 25:15-26).

And Babylon, the glory of kingdoms, the beauty of the Chaldees excellency, shall be as when God overthrew Sodom and Gomorrah (Isa. 13:19).

Idolatry is called fornication and spiritual adultery. Babylon is brought before us in chapter 17. This verse is but an announcement of coming events.

d. **PRONOUNCEMENT** of Judgment on Those Who Received the Mark of the Beast, verses 9-12

Verses 9-12—And the third angel followed them, saying with a loud voice, If any man worship the beast and his image, and receive his mark in his forehead, or in his hand, the same shall drink of the wine of the wrath of God, which is poured out without mixture into the cup of his indignation; and he shall be tormented with fire and brimstone in the presence of the holy angels, and in the presence of the Lamb: and the smoke of their torment ascendeth up for ever and ever: and they have no rest day nor night, who worship the beast and his image, and whosoever receiveth the mark of his name. Here is the patience of the saints: here are they that keep the commandments of God, and the faith of Jesus.

And another angel, a third, followed them, saying with a great voice, If any man worshippeth the beast and his image, and receiveth a mark on his forehead, or upon his hand, he also shall drink of the wine of the wrath of God, which is mingled unmixed in the cup of His anger; and he shall be tormented with fire and brimstone in the presence of the holy angels, and in the presence of the Lamb; and the smoke of their torment goeth up for ever and ever (unto the ages of the ages); and they have no rest day and night, they that worship the wild beast and his image, and whoso receiveth the mark of his name.

25

(Here is) the patience of the saints, who keep the commandments of God and the faith of Jesus.

This section makes it crystal clear that no one can assume a neutral position during this intense period under the Beast. Even today we see Christian business men who are capitulating to the ethics of the hour. In chapter 13 we saw that the awful alternative for refusing to receive the mark of the Beast was starvation. On the other hand, the person who receives the mark, brings down upon his head the wrath of God.

He shall drink of the wine of the wrath of God is a figure adopted from the Old Testament:

> For in the hand of the LORD there is a cup, and the wine is red; it is full of mixture; and he poureth out of the same: but the dregs thereof, all the wicked of the earth shall wring them out, and drink them (Psa. 75:8).

The Old Testament saw the cup of wrath filling up to the brim, and then saw God pressing it to the lips of a godless society.

Tormented with fire and brimstone if not literal is something ten times worse. Remember that the brimstone of Sodom was literal.

Hell is visible to Christ and the holy angels. It does not say that it is visible to the 24 elders. Are we to assume from that that the Church does not know what is taking place on the earth?

All that God's own can do in this period is to be patient and wait for the coming of Christ (see chapter 13:10). Our Lord said: "But he that shall endure unto the end, the same shall be saved" (Matt. 24:13); "In your patience possess ye your souls" (Luke 21:19).

e. PRAISE for Those Who Die in the Lord, verse 13

Verse 13—And I heard a voice from heaven saying unto me, Write, Blessed are the dead which die in the Lord from henceforth: Yea, saith the Spirit, that they may rest from their labours; and their works do follow them.

And I heard a voice from heaven saying, Write, Blessed are the dead who die in the Lord from henceforth: yea, said the Spirit, that they may rest from their labors (sorrows), for their works follow with them.

This is not a statement for saints in the present age. For believers to want to die is unnatural:

> For I am in a strait betwixt two, having a desire to depart, and to be with Christ; which is far better: nevertheless to abide in the flesh is more needful for you. And having this confidence, I know that I shall abide and continue with you all for your furtherance and joy of faith; that your rejoicing may be more abundant in Jesus Christ for me by my coming to you again. (Phil 1:23-26).

During the Great Tribulation, however, it will be better to die than to live. At that time verse 13 will give comfort and assurance.

That they may rest from their labors shows the awful pressure upon the bodies and minds of God's own in this time of intensity. It is best to leave the world in this period.

For their works follow with them reveals that they will be rewarded for their faithfulness, patience and works in this period. God does not save anyone for his works, but He does reward us for our works. Our works (good or bad) are like tin cans tied to a dog's tail—we can't get away from them. They will follow us to the Bema Seat of Christ.

f. **PREVIEW** of Armageddon, verses 14-20

Verse 14—And I looked, and behold a white cloud, and upon the cloud one sat like unto the Son of man, having on his head a golden crown, and in his hand a sharp sickle.

And I saw, and behold, a white cloud; and on the cloud one sitting like unto a Son of man, having on His head a golden crown and in His hand a sharp sickle.

And I saw, and behold emphasizes that John is still an auditor.

A white cloud, and on the cloud one sitting like unto a Son of man is evidently the Lord Jesus Christ—although it is well to note that article is *a* son, not *the* son. In Revelation 1:13, *a* Son of man is Christ (see our translation). The cloud is a mark of identification:

> And then shall appear the sign of the Son of man in heaven: and then shall all the tribes of the earth mourn, and they shall see the Son of man coming in the clouds of heaven with power and great glory (Matt. 24:30).

> Behold, he cometh with clouds; and every eye shall see him, and they also which pierced him: and all kindreds of the earth shall wail because of him. Even so, Amen (Rev. 1:7).

On His head a golden crown further confirms this One as the Lord Jesus Christ. He is seen as king here—not prophet or priest. His office as king is connected with His return to earth.

The *sharp sickle* establishes this and speaks of the judgment of the wicked. Dr. Newell calls attention to the occurrences of the word *sickle*. He notes that it occurs only 12 times in the Scriptures, of which 7 are in the verses of this section. Also the word *sharp* occurs 7 times in the Revelation — 4 times here.

Verses 15, 16—And another angel came out of the temple, crying with a loud voice to him that sat on the cloud, Thrust in thy sickle, and reap: for the time is come for thee to reap; for the harvest of the earth is ripe. And he that sat on the cloud thrust in his sickle on the earth; and the earth was reaped.

And another angel came out of the temple, crying in a great voice to the One seated on the cloud. Send forth thy sickle, and reap; for the hour is come to reap; for the harvest of the earth was dried. And He that sat on the cloud cast his sickle upon (epi - *against*) *the earth; and the earth was reaped.*

Send forth thy sickle, and reap refers to the judgment of men on the earth (see Matt. 13:40-42). In Matthew the "harvest" has so long been identified with Christian witnessing, and believers have been urged to pray for laborers for the harvest, that it is difficult for the average Christian to fit this scene into the true context of Scripture. Actually, believers are urged to sow seed, not to harvest (see Matt. 13:3-9; I Cor. 3:5-8). Jesus gave instructions to pray for laborers to enter the harvest at the end of the age of law (see Matt. 9:38). This is the promised word of the Father to the Son as given in Psalm 2:7-9:

> I will declare the decree: the LORD hath said unto me, Thou art my Son; this day have I begotten thee. Ask of me, and I shall give thee the heathen for thine inheritance, and the uttermost parts of the earth for thy possession. Thou shalt break them with a rod of iron; thou shalt dash them in pieces like a potter's vessel.

For the hour is come to reap is in conformity to the words of Jesus, "the harvest is the end of the age" (Matt. 13:39).

> Put ye in the sickle, for the harvest is ripe; come, get you down; for the press is full, the fats overflow; for their wickedness is great. Multitudes, multitudes in the valley of decision: for the day of the LORD is near in the valley of decision (Joel 3:13, 14).

For the harvest of the earth was dried reveals the awful spiritual deadness which merits judgment.

> For if they do these things in a green tree, what shall be done in the dry? (Luke 23:31).

And the earth was reaped is the finis to man's vaunted civilization. This is the outcome of the battle of Armageddon.

Verses 17, 18—And another angel came out of the temple which is in heaven, he also having a sharp sickle. And another angel came out from the altar, which had power over fire; and cried with a loud cry to him that had the sharp sickle, saying, Thrust in thy sharp sickle, and gather the clusters of the vine of the earth; for her grapes are fully ripe.

And another angel came out from the sanctuary (temple) which is in heaven, he also having a sharp sickle. And another angel came out from the altar, he that hath (having) power over the fire, and he called with a great voice to him that had the sharp sickle, saying, Send forth thy sharp sickle, and gather the clusters of the vine of the earth; for her grapes are fully ripe.

And another angel merely identifies another messenger of God who is faceless and nameless. These are the angels who assist Christ in the work of judgment at His coming:

> So shall it be at the end of the world: the angels shall come forth, and sever the wicked from among the just (Matt. 13:49).

Sanctuary (temple) which is in heaven (see 11:19).

A sharp sickle points to judgment.

Hath power over the fire intensifies the thought content of judgment.

Gather the clusters of the vine of the earth; for the grapes are fully ripe contains the thought that the grapes are dry (raisins). This is a change of metaphor for the Battle of Armageddon, and is strictly scriptural:

> For their vine is of the vine of Sodom, and of the fields of Gomorrah: their grapes are grapes of gall, their clusters are bitter: their wine is the poison of dragons, and the cruel venom of asps. Is not this laid up in store with me, and sealed up among my treasures?

To me belongeth vengeance, and recompence; their foot shall slide in due time: for the day of their calamity is at hand, and the things that shall come upon them make haste (Deut. 32:32-35).

The figure is identical to the one in that awe-inspiring chapter of Isaiah:
Who is this that cometh from Edom, with dyed garments from Bozrah? this that is glorious in his apparel, travelling in the greatness of his strength I that speak in righteousness, mighty to save. Wherefore art thou red in thine apparel, and thy garments like him that treadeth in the winefat? I have trodden the winepress alone; and of the people there was none with me: for I will tread them in mine anger, and trample them in my fury; and their blood shall be sprinkled upon my garments, and I will stain all my raiment. For the day of vengeance is in mine heart, and the year of my redeemed is come. And I looked, and there was none to help; and I wondered that there was none to uphold: therefore mine own arm brought salvation unto me; and my fury, it upheld me. And I will tread down the people in mine anger, and make them drunk in my fury, and I will bring down their strength to the earth (Isa. 63:1-6).

This is a picture of Christ coming to the battle of Armageddon (see Rev. 19: 11-21 and Joel 3:9-16).

And he gathered them together into a place called in the Hebrew tongue Armageddon (Rev. 16:16).

Verses 19, 20—And the angel thrust in his sickle into the earth, and gathered the vine of the earth, and cast it into the great winepress of the wrath of God. And the winepress was trodden without the city, and blood came out of the winepress, even unto the horse bridles, by the space of a thousand and six hundred furloughs.

And the angel cast his sickle into the earth, and gathered the vine of the earth, and cast it into the winepress, the great winepress of the wrath of God. And the winepress was trodden without the city, and there came out blood from the winepress, even unto the bridles of the horses, as far as a thousand and six hundred furlongs.

This is one of the most awe-inspiring pictures depicted on the pages of Scripture. It describes the same scene as does Isaiah 63 where He is seen treading the winepress alone. It is positively terrifying. Little wonder that the men of the earth cried to the rocks to fall upon them and hide them from the wrath of the Lamb. This is the sad end of that civilization which, at the tower of Babel, demonstrated an active rebellion against God, which has been mounting up like a mighty crescendo ever since. This scene is given also in Isaiah 34:

Come near, ye nations, to hear; and hearken, ye people: let the earth hear, and all that is therein; the world, and all things that come forth of it. For the indignation of the LORD is upon all nations, and his fury upon all their armies; he hath utterly destroyed them, he hath delivered them to the slaughter. Their slain also shall be cast out, and their stink shall come up out of their carcasses, and the mountains shall be melted with their blood. . . . The sword of the LORD is filled with blood, it is made fat with fatness, and with the blood of lambs and goats, with the fat of the kidneys of rams: for the LORD hath a sacrifice in Bozrah, and a great slaughter in the land of Idumea (Isa. 34:1-3, 6).

The *precious blood* of the Lamb having been rejected, the blood of those who defied God and followed and worshipped the Beast bathes the earth. It is frightful. As a ripe grape is mashed and the juice flies in every direction, so will little man fall into the vat of God's judgment. This is Armageddon—the mount of slaughter.

Without the city means without Jerusalem.

Unto the bridles of the horses means about three or four feet deep.

A thousand and six hundred furlongs is about 185 miles. A furlong or stadium was 606¾ English feet. It is the length of about 1600 football fields. More accurately it is 183.8 miles, which is about the distance from Dan to Beersheba. All of Palestine is the scene of this final battle. It is a campaign beginning about the middle of the Great Tribulation and concluded by the personal return of Christ to the earth.

> Gird thy sword upon thy thigh, O most mighty, with thy glory and thy majesty. And in thy majesty ride prosperously because of truth and meekness and righteousness; and thy right hand shall teach thee terrible things. Thine arrows are sharp in the heart of the king's enemies; whereby the people fall under thee. Thy throne O God, is for ever and ever: the sceptre of thy kingdom is a right sceptre. Thou lovest righteousness, and hatest wickedness: therefore God, thy God, hath anointed thee with the oil of gladness above thy fellows (Psa. 45:3-7).

I make no apology for this scene—God has not asked me to do so. We need to face up to the facts:

1. Sin is an awful thing.
2. Sin is in the world.
3. You and I are sinners.
4. You and I merit the judgment of God. Our only escape is to accept the blood Christ shed for us on Calvary's cross. "How shall we escape if we neglect so great salvation?" We cannot escape. This judgment must inevitably come on Christ rejecters. Men have rejected Him and treated His sacrifice as an unclean thing, and have trodden under foot the Son of God. If God is just (and He is) there will be judgment.

Chapter 15

THEME: Another Sign in Heaven, Seven Angels with the Seven Last Plagues

OUTLINE:

5. **Pouring Out of the Seven Mixing Bowls of Wrath,** chapters 15, 16

   a. Preparation for the Final Judgment of the Great Tribulation,
   15:1 - 16:1

      (1) Tribulation Saints in Heaven Worship God Because He is Holy and Just, 15:1-4

      (2) Temple of the Tabernacle Opened in Heaven that Seven Angels, Having Seven Golden Bowls, Might Proceed Forth, 15:5-16:1

   b. Pouring Out of the **First** Bowl, 16:2

   c. Pouring Out of the **Second** Bowl, 16:3

   d. Pouring Out of the **Third** Bowl, 16:4-7

   e. Pouring Out of the **Fourth** Bowl, 16:8, 9

   f. Pouring Out of the **Fifth** Bowl, 16:10, 11

   g. Pouring Out of the **Sixth** Bowl, 16:12

   h. Interlude: Kings of Inhabited Earth Proceed to Har-Magedon, 16:13-16

   i. Pouring Out of the **Seventh** Bowl, 16:17-21

REMARKS:

As the outline indicates, chapters 15 and 16 belong together. Chapter 15, besides being the shortest chapter in Revelation, is the preface to the final series of judgments which come on the earth during the Great Tribulation. These judgments are the most intense and devastating of any that have preceded them.

Before these angels begin to pour out their bowls of wrath, there may be the question still in the minds of some if any were able to stand up against Antichrist. If that question has not been answered to the satisfaction of the reader, it is answered here.

COMMENT:

a. Preparation for the Final Judgment of the Great Tribulation,
15:1 - 16:1

   (1) Tribulation Saints in Heaven Worship God Because He is Holy and Just, 15:1-4

Verse 1—And I saw another sign in heaven, great and marvelous, seven angels having the seven last plagues; for in them is filled up the wrath of God.

And I saw another sign in (the) heaven, great and wonderful. seven angels having seven plagues, which are the last, for in them (was) finished the wrath of God.

And I saw assures us that John is still a spectator to these events. He is attending the dress rehearsal of the last act of man's little day upon the earth.

Another sign connects this chapter with Revelation 12:1, the first sign, which was Israel. These seven angels of wrath are connected with the judgments to follow—until Christ comes (chapter 19). From chapter 12 to the Return of Christ is a series of events which are mutually related. This does not mean that there is a chronological order, but rather a retracing of the same events with added detail. This method is the personal signature of the Holy Spirit, seen first in Genesis 1 and 2. It is known as the law of recapitulation (see author's, *Going Through Genesis*, p. 6).

Satan being cast into the earth brings down his wrath upon the remnant of Israel. Also he makes a final thrust for world domination through the two Beasts. Then God makes a final display of His wrath, and concludes earth's sordid tragedy of sin.

> The LORD said unto my Lord, Sit thou at my right hand, until I make thine enemies thy footstool (Psa. 110:1).

Was finished in the Greek is the prophetic aorist, which considers an event in the future as already acomplished.

The wrath of God marks the final judgment of the Great Tribulation. God has been slow to anger; but here ends His longsuffering. Judgment, in the final stages of the Day of Wrath, proceeds from God—not from Satan nor the Wild Beast.

Verse 2—And I saw as it were a sea of glass mingled with fire: and them that had gotten the victory over the beast, and over his image, and over his mark, and over the number of his name, stand on the sea of glass, having the harps of God.

And I saw as it were a glassy sea mingled with fire, and them that came off victorious from the wild beast, and from his image, and from the number of his name, standing by (on the shore of) the glassy sea, having harps of God.

The glassy sea mingled with fire is *the frightful persecution of the Beast.*

And them that came off victorious—here are the tribulation saints who have come through the fires of persecution on the earth, yet have not lost their song. Are you having trouble keeping from your heart a little root of bitterness? We need to pray, in the face of life's circumstances, that a root of bitterness will not spring up. It is interesting to see that these tribulation saints, who have lived through the tribulation, have kept their song.

> For his anger endureth but a moment; in his favor is life: weeping may endure for a night, but joy cometh in the morning (Psa. 30:5).

Verses 3,4—And they sing the song of Moses the servant of God, and the song of the Lamb, saying, Great and marvellous are thy works, Lord God Almighty; just and true are thy ways, thou King of saints. Who shall not fear thee, O Lord, and glorify thy name? for thou only art holy: for all nations shall come and worship before thee; for thy judgments are made manifest.

And they sing the song of Moses the servant of God, and the song of the Lamb, saying, Great and wonderful are thy works, Lord God, the Almighty; righteous and true are thy ways, thou King of the ages (nations). Who shall not fear, Lord, and glorify thy name? For thou only art holy; for all the na-

tions shall come and worship before thee; for thy righteous acts were made manifest.

If you want to learn *the song of Moses,* you will find it in Exodus 15:1-21 and Deuteronomy 32:1-43. Both songs speak of God's deliverance, salvation, and faithfulness. The song of the Lamb is the ascription of praise to Christ, as the Redeemer (see Revelation 5:9-12). The book of Revelation is Christo-centric. Christ directs all things; and He is the object of worship. Remember that this book is the "unveiling of Jesus Christ."

In the verse before us, the two songs merge into a universal chorus.

King of the ages has two other renderings, *King of saints* and *King of the nations.* Any rendering indicates that Christ will be the object of universal worship and acknowledgment. There will be no place where He will not be worshipped.

Who shall not fear, Lord, and glorify thy name? In our day there is very little reverential fear of God. However, God is moving in on churches and dealing with Christians as He never has done before. If you are God's child you had better not do as you please. If you think God would mind sending you trouble, you are wrong. God is to be feared.

Nations shall come and worship before thee. The day will come when nations will come and worship before Him. This knowledge causes us to take heart as we see our own nation moving in the wrong direction today.

Ask of me, and I shall give thee the heathen for thine inheritance, and the uttermost parts of the earth for thy possession (Psa. 2:8).

They shall not hurt nor destroy in all my holy mountain: for the earth shall be full of the knowledge of the LORD, as the waters cover the sea (Isa. 11:9).

Behold, the days come, saith the LORD, that I will raise unto David a righteous Branch, and a King shall reign and prosper, and shall execute judgment and justice in the earth (Jer. 23:5).

Wherefore God also hath highly exalted him, and given him a name which is above every name: that at the name of Jesus every knee should bow, of things in heaven, and things in earth, and things under the earth; and that every tongue should confess that Jesus Christ is Lord, to the glory of God the Father (Phil. 2:9-11).

Thy righteous acts comes from the lips of those who passed through the Great Tribulation. This testimony, coming from witnesses of this period, is in-expressibly impressive, and should settle in the minds of believers the fact that God is right in all that He does.

Oh let the wickedness of the wicked come to an end; but establish the just: for the righteous God trieth the hearts and reins (Psa. 7:9).

For the righteous LORD loveth righteousness; his countenance doth behold the upright (Psa. 11:7).

O give thanks unto the LORD, for he is good: for his mercy en-dureth for ever . . . . He poureth contempt upon princes, and causeth them to wander in the wilderness, where there is no way . . . . The righteous shall see it, and rejoice: and all iniquity shall stop her mouth (Psa. 107: 1, 40, 42).

33

(2) Temple of the Tabernacle Opened in Heaven that Seven Angels, Having Seven Golden Bowls, Might Proceed Forth, 15:5-16:1

Verses 5, 6—And after that I looked, and, behold, the temple of the tabernacle of the testimony in heaven was opened: and the seven angels came out of the temple, having the seven plagues, clothed in pure and white linen, and having their breasts girded with golden girdles.

And after these things I saw, and the sanctuary (temple) of the tabernacle (skenes) of the testimony (witness) in (the) heaven was opened; and there came out from the temple (the) seven angels, having the seven plagues, clothed in linen (precious stone) pure and white, and girt about the breast with golden girdles.

The temple is referred to fifteen (15) times in the Revelation. Its prominence cannot be ignored. Each reference is either to the temple in heaven or to the absence of the temple in the New Jerusalem. In this instance the reference is specifically to the Tabernacle *(skenes)*, and the Holy of Holies in which the ark of the testimony was kept. In the ark were the tables of stone. Both the tabernacle and the tables of stone were duplicates of originals in heaven.

> And look that thou . make them after their pattern, which was shewed thee in the mount (Ex. 25:40).

> It was therefore necessary that the patterns of things in the heavens should be purified with these; but the heavenly things themselves with better sacrifices than these (Heb. 9:23).

The originals are referred to in Revelation 11:19. The action of God here is based on the violation of His covenant with Israel—the broken law. God is righteous in what He is about to do. He will judge, then He will carry out His covenant with Israel.

The prominence of angels in this book is again called to our attention by the appearance of angels at this point. Previously seven angels blew on seven trumpets. Here is a new series of seven, who have the seven last plagues (bowls of wrath).

Their departure from the temple demonstrates that they have departed from the mercy seat and now God acts in justice and not mercy.

Clothed in linen (precious stone) is an enigmatic expression, due to a variant reading in the text. Were they clothed in linen or a stone? The intention, it seems, is to describe their garments as studded and set with precious stones. Though their garments identify them in a priestly activity, they forsake that work of mercy for plagues of judgment.

The *golden girdles* reveal them in the livery of Christ (1:13), who no longer is exercising a priestly function, but is seen here judging the world.

Verses 7, 8—And one of the four beasts gave unto the seven angels golden vials full of the wrath of God, who liveth for ever and ever. And the temple was filled with smoke from the glory of God, and from his power; and no man was able to enter into the temple, till the seven plagues of the seven angels were fulfilled.

And one of the four living creatures gave to the seven angels seven golden bowls, full of the wrath of God, who liveth for ever and ever. And the sanctu-

ary (temple) was filled with smoke from the glory of God, and from his power; and no one was able to enter into the sanctuary (temple), till the seven plagues of the seven angels should be finishd.

Seven golden bowls represent the final tribulation. *Bowls* better describe the containers than does the word *vials*. Bowls were used in the temple service. A bowl of blood was taken by the high priest one day each year into the Holy of Holies. The bowl of blood spoke of redemption for sin. These seven angels with priestly garments, having departed from the temple proper, are no longer engaged in a service of mercy, but are beginning a strange ministry—pouring out bowls of wrath on a Christ-rejecting world. A world that has rejected the blood of Christ, must bear the judgment for sin. This judgment is not the result of man's or Satan's enmity. It is the direct action of the Lord Jesus Christ. The first three bowls have to do with blood; the first reveals the bad blood of men—"noisome and grievous sore."

The prophets used the figure of the cup of iniquity and wrath which would be finally poured out in judgment. (See Psa. 11:6; Isa. 51:17; Jer. 25:15; Ezek. 23:33; Hab. 2:16.)

Smoke is connected with the glory of God. (See Ex. 40:34; I Kings 8:10; Psa. 18:8; Isa. 6:4.) The glory of the Lord was manifested in the pillar of cloud and smoke. Always the glory of the Lord manifested itself in time of judgment. God is going to maintain His glory; He does not intend to let any of His creatures get by with sin. If you have been complacently living in sin, thinking you are getting by with it, I have news for you. He is never in a hurry, the cup is filling up. If He does not judge you today, He always has tomorrow.

These seven angels with seven golden bowls make it clear that the judgments of the bowls proceed from God and are not the result of man's miscalculations or of Satan's enmity.

Chapter 16

THEME: The Seven Angels pour out the Seven Bowls of the wrath of God upon the earth.

OUTLINE: (See chapter 15)

REMARKS:

This chapter contains the record of the pouring out of all seven bowls of wrath—including the interlude between the 6th and 7th bowls. Chapter 15 is the preliminary section and the prelude to this chapter, and is organically connected with it.

It is worth repeating to again state that the bowls of wrath contain the direct judgment of God upon the world; they do not proceed from either man's misdoings or Satan's machinations. They are poured out during the reign of the beast (verse 1). They cover a very brief period of time, comparatively speaking.

There is a definite similarity between the judgments in this chapter and God's judgments upon Egypt through Moses.

COMMENT:

a. Preparation for Final Judgment of the Great Tribulation, 15:1-16:1

Verse 1—And I heard a great voice out of the temple saying to the seven angels, Go your ways, and pour out the vials of the wrath of God upon the earth.

And I heard a great voice out of the sanctuary (temple) saying to the seven angels, Go and pour out the seven bowls of the wrath of God into the earth.

In this book, the Lord Jesus Christ is in complete charge and control. The Father has committed all judgment unto Him. He gives the command. There is no longer delay, interval, or intermission. The hour has come, the order is given and the seven angels execute the command.

It is difficult for man, even Christians, to believe that God is going to pour out His wrath on a rebellious and God-hating world, and destroy this civilization. After almost a century of insipid preaching from America's pulpits, the average man believes God is all sweetness and light, and would not discipline or punish anyone.

b. Pouring Out of the FIRST BOWL, verse 2

Verse 2—And the first went, and poured out his vial upon the earth; and there fell a noisome and grievous sore upon the men which had the mark of the beast, and upon them which worshipped his image.

And the first went and poured out his bowl into the earth; and it became (there broke out) a noisome and grievous sore upon the men that had the mark of the wild beast, and that worshipped his image.

Vincent writes, "Each angel, as his turn comes, withdraws from the heavenly scene."

God is engaged in germ warfare upon the followers of Antichrist. Scripture states that the life of the flesh is in the blood, and also death is in the blood.

36

These putrifying sores are worse than leprosy or cancer. As man discovers a remedy for one disease, another that is more frightful appears. These are judgments of God, by which He reveals physically what man is morally—utterly corrupt.

This compares to the sixth plague in Egypt, and is the same type of sore or "boil" (see Exodus 9:8-12). It is interesting to note that Moses predicted a judgment upon Israel, similar to this, which has not as yet been fulfilled (see Deuteronomy 28:15, 27, 35).

c. Pouring Out of the SECOND BOWL, verse 3

Verse 3—And the second angel poured out his vial upon the sea; and it became as the blood of a dead man: and every living soul died in the sea.

And the second poured out his bowl into the sea; and it became (there came) blood as of a dead man; and every living soul (soul of life) died, even the things in the sea.

This plague is more severe than that of the second trumpet, where only one third of the sea became blood (8:8, 9). Here it is the total sea, and the blood is as of a dead man. Blood is the token of life, "The life of the flesh is in the blood." The sea is a great reservoir of life. It is teeming with life and the salty water is a cathartic for the filth of the earth. However, in this plague blood is the token of death; the sea becomes a grave of death instead of a womb of life. The cool sea breezes become a stench from the carcasses floating on the surface of the water (that is now bloody) and lining the shore. Commerce is paralyzed. Human beings die like flies. The first plague in Egypt was the turning of the waters of the Nile into blood (Exodus 7:20-25).

Do we actually realize how much we are dependent on God today? The light company, the gas company, the water company send us bills—but where did they get the light, the gas and the water? Has *God* ever sent you a bill for the sunshine, for the water you drink and the air you breathe? Have you paid Him? He has not sent His bill, and you would not be able to pay it if He did. God who has been so gracious to a Christ-rejecting world will at last judge all the earth. The angels pour out the bowls in the day of God's wrath.

d. Pouring Out of the THIRD BOWL, verses 4-7

Verses 4-7—And the third angel poured out his vial upon the rivers and fountains of waters; and they became blood. And I heard the angel of the waters say, Thou art righteous, O Lord, which art, and wast, and shalt be, because thou hast judged thus. For they have shed the blood of saints and prophets, and thou hast given them blood to drink; for they are worthy. And I heard another out of the altar say, Even so, Lord God Almighty, true and righteous are thy judgments.

And the third poured out his bowl into the rivers and the fountains of the waters and it became (there came) blood. And I heard the angel of the waters saying, Righteous art thou, who art and who wast, The Holy One, because thou didst judge these things. For they shed the blood of saints and prophets, and blood didst thou give them to drink; they are worthy. And I heard the altar saying, Yea, the Lord God, the Almighty, true and righteous are thy judgments.

This plague, similar to that of the third trumpet, again is more severe. There one third of the fresh water was affected. Here the total water supply of the earth will be cut off. This means destruction of human life on an unparalleled plane.

The angel of the waters is the superintendent of God's water department here on earth. This reveals another ministry of angels as it affects creation. They are in charge of the physical universe. We have seen the four angels who control the winds. This angel, who knows the whole story now declares that God is right and holy in this act of judgment.

They shed the blood of the saints and prophets, and blood didst thou give them to drink. Such is poetic justice with a vengeance. Those who take the sword will perish with the sword; and the shedding of blood leads to the shedding of blood. These, who are being judged, made martyrs of God's people, and now God is forcing them to drink blood for the righteous blood they spilled.

The altar saying evidently refers back to the saints under the altar who had been praying for justice to be done (6:9-11). Here their prayer is answered and they declare that God is true and righteous. All creatures will agree that God is right in these judgments. Only man, who today is in rebellion against God, disagrees. There is no place of safety out of Christ. He is, as was the ark in Noah's day, the only safe place.

e. Pouring Out of the **FOURTH BOWL,** verses 8, 9

Verses 8, 9—And the fourth angel poured out his vial upon the sun; and power was given unto him to scorch men with fire. And men were scorched with great heat, and blasphemed the name of God, which hath power over these plagues: and they repented not to give him glory.

And the fourth poured out his bowl upon the sun; and it was given to it to scorch (the) men with (in) fire. And (the) men were scorched with great heat; and they blasphemed the name of God who hath the power over these plagues, and they repented not to give Him glory.

Our Lord predicted signs in the sun during the Great Tribulation:

And there shall be signs in the sun, and in the moon, and in the stars; and upon the earth distress of nations, with perplexity; the sea and the waves roaring (Luke 21:25).

The Old Testament had a great deal to say about judgment in the Great Tribulation due to the excessive heat of the sun:

They shall be burnt with hunger, and devoured with burning heat, and with bitter destruction: I will also send the teeth of beasts upon them, with the poison of serpents of the dust (Deut. 32:24).

Therefore hath the curse devoured the earth, and they that dwell therein are desolate: therefore the inhabitants of the earth are burned, and few men left (Isa. 24:6).

Therefore he hath poured upon him the fury of his anger, and the strength of battle: and it hath set him on fire round about, yet he knew not; and it burned him, yet he laid it not to heart (Isa 42:25).

For, behold, the day cometh, that shall burn as an oven; and all the proud, yea, and all that do wickedly, shall be stubble: and the day that cometh shall burn them up, saith the LORD of hosts, that it shall leave them neither root nor branch (Mal. 4:1).

All the Lord would have to do is to remove one or two blankets of atmosphere, or pull the earth a little closer to the sun. It will be a frightful period in which, as Isaiah states, the earth will be decimated. Read Isaiah 24. Our Lord's language assumes new meaning in the light of this plague, "Except those days should be shortened, there should no flesh be saved."

Nevertheless, His own are preserved; "The sun shall not smite thee by day, nor the moon by night" (Psalm 121:6). Though this promise is quite meaningless to us today, it will be a great comfort to the believer in the Great Tribulation.

And men . . . blasphemed the name of God shows that the human heart is incurable, and no amount of punishment will purify and change it.

And repented not to give Him glory. "The heart is desperately wicked" tells the frightful story of man—of which this is the proof.

At the fourth trumpet the sun, moon, and stars were smitten to the extent that one third was darkened. Here the heat of the sun is intensified.

f. Pouring Out of the FIFTH BOWL, verses 10, 11

Verses 10, 11—And the fifth angel poured out his vial upon the seat of the beast; and his kingdom was full of darkness; and they gnawed their tongues for pain, and blasphemed the God of heaven because of their pains and their sores, and repented not of their deeds.

And the fifth poured out his bowl upon the throne of the wild beast; and his kingdom was darkened, and they chewed their tongues from their pain, and they blasphemed the God of heaven because of their pains and their sores; and they repented not of their works.

The throne of the wild beast confirms the accuracy of our interpretation of the Wild Beast (in Revelation 13) being a man. We believe that the location of his throne is Babylon, as will be shown in the next two chapters.

His kingdom was darkened indicates a strange darkness which might be called "black light." It is a frightening thing, as the sun's wattage is increased during this period. The heat will be greater but the light will be less. There is a remarkable similarity to the darkness in Egypt during the 9th plague (Exodus 10:21, 22).

The Old Testament prophets had a great deal to say about this coming darkness:

For, behold, the darkness shall cover the earth, and gross darkness the people: but the LORD shall arise upon thee, and his glory shall be seen upon thee (Isa. 60:2).

Blow ye the trumpet in Zion, and sound an alarm in my holy mountain: let all the inhabitants of the land tremble: for the day of the LORD cometh, for it is nigh at hand; a day of darkness and of gloominess, a day of clouds and of thick darkness, as the morning spread upon the mountains: a great people and a strong; there hath not been ever the like, neither shall be any more after it, even to the years of many generations. . . . The sun shall be turned into darkness, and the moon into blood, before the great and the terrible day of the LORD come (Joel 2:1, 2, 31).

Who can stand before his indignation? and who can abide in the fierceness of his anger? his fury is poured out like fire, and the rocks are thrown down by him . . . But with an overrunning flood he will make an utter end of the place thereof, and darkness shall pursue his enemies (Nahum 1:6, 8).

Woe unto you that desire the day of the LORD! to what end is it for you? the day of the LORD is darkness, and not light (Amos 5:18).

That day is a day of wrath, a day of trouble and distress, a day of wasteness and desolation, a day of darkness and gloominess, a day of clouds and thick darkness (Zeph. 1:15)

Our Lord confirmed it:

But in those days, after that tribulation, the sun shall be darkened, and the moon shall not give her light (Mark 13:24).

They chewed their tongues from their pain reveals the intensity of suffering caused by all the bowls of wrath which are poured out in rapid succession so that they descend like a mighty flood striking almost simultaneously.

There are two self-evident facts at this point:

(1) God is righteous in pouring out the bowls of wrath (remember, Jesus is the judge);

(2) Men are not led to repentance by suffering.

Or despisest thou the riches of his goodness and forbearance and longsuffering; not knowing that the goodness of God leadeth thee to repentance? But after thy hardness and impenitent heart treasurest up unto thyself wrath against the day of wrath and revelation of the righteous judgment of God (Rom. 2:4, 5).

g. Pouring Out of the SIXTH BOWL, verse 12

Verse 12—And the sixth angel poured out his vial upon the great river Euphrates; and the water thereof was dried up, that the way of the kings of the east might be prepared.

And the sixth poured out his bowl upon the great river, the river Euphrates; and the water was dried up, that the way might be made ready for the kings that come from the sunrising.

The Euphrates is called "the great river" (see Deuteronomy 1:7), as the Mediterranean Sea was called "the great sea." The prominence of the Euphrates River in the Word of God should not be overlooked. First mentioned in Genesis 2, it is designated over 25 times in the Bible. In the verse before us it is seen in connection with the sixth plague. As it was prominent in the first state of man on the earth, so is it featured in his last state—that of the Great Tribulation. It was the cradle of man's civilization, and obviously will be the grave of man's civilization. It was a border between east and west, flowing

1800 miles long, over half of it navigable. It is wide and deep, which makes it difficult for an army to pass over it.

Abraham was called a Hebrew, and some interpret that as meaning he came from the other side of the Euphrates.

The Euphrates was the eastern border of the land promised to Abraham:

> In the same day the LORD made a covenant with Abram, saying, Unto thy seed have I given this land, from the river of Egypt unto the great river, the river Euphrates (Gen. 15:18).

> From the wilderness and this Lebanon even unto the great river, the river Euphrates, all of the land of the Hittites, and unto the great sea toward the going down of the sun, shall be your coast (Josh. 1:4).

It became also the eastern border of the Roman Empire.

The Euphrates will be miraculously dried up, thus erasing the border of east and west, that the kings of the sunrising might come to the battle of Armageddon.

The bulk of the population is in the Orient. These great hordes, that have never before moved west, now come on a great crusade to Palestine. Having had a smattering of the Gospel, they choose Antichrist, and move out of the east across the Euphrates. The picture is frightful. Can anyone doubt, with hundreds of millions pouring into Palestine, that the blood will be up to the horse bridles?

h. Interlude: Kings of Inhabited Earth Proceed to Har-Magedon, verses 13-16

Verses 13, 14—And I saw three unclean spirits like frogs come out of the mouth of the dragon, and out of the mouth of the beast, and out of the mouth of the false prophet. For they are the spirits of devils, working miracles, which go forth unto the kings of the earth and of the whole world, to gather them to the battle of that great day of God Almighty.

And I saw (coming) out of the mouth of the dragon, and out of the mouth of the wild beast, and out of the mouth of the false prophet, as it were frogs. For they are spirits of demons, working signs; which go forth upon the kings of the whole inhabited earth, to gather them together to the war of the great day of the God, the Almighty.

Between the 6th and 7th bowl of wrath is this interlude. (An interlude is the regular occurance between the 6th and 7th features of each series of seven—the seven performers being the one exception where it occurs after the 7th performer). It brings up for us Har-Magedon, which is not a single battle but a war called Har-Magedon. It will be triggered by the coming down of Russia from the north sometime around the middle of the tribulation period. The campaign extends the length of Palestine to the Valley of Jehoshaphat and the mountains of Edom. It will continue for approximately 3½ years. It will be concluded by the Lord Jesus Christ coming from heaven to establish His kingdom—the Sun of righteousness will arise with healing in his wings.

Here is introduced the trinity of hell—Satan, Antichrist and the false prophet. They act in unison in forcing the nations of the world to march against Israel in an attempt to destroy God's purposes on the earth.

41

As it were frogs reminds us again of the second plague in Egypt which the magicians of Egypt, Jannes and Jambres, duplicated:

And the magicians did so with their enchantments, and brought up frogs upon the land of Egypt (Exodus 8:7).

However, John says, *as it were* frogs, indicating that a symbol is being used. While we believe they are symbolic, we do not rule out the possibility that they are literal frogs.

These miracles serve to convince the kings of the earth, and to deceive the world. Our Lord predicted this very thing:

For there shall arise false Christs, and false prophets, and shall show great signs and wonders; insomuch that, if it were possible, they shall deceive the very elect (Matt. 24:24).

It is impossible for us to determine their strategy. Frogs are an apt picture of what will go forth as the Great Lie. Seiss describes them in this vivid manner:

They are spirits; they are "unclean spirits;" they are "demon spirits;" they are sent forth into activity by the Dragon Trinity; they are the elect agents to awaken the world to the attempt to abolish God from the earth; and they are frog-like in that they come forth out of the pestiferous quagmires of the universe, do their work amid the world's evening shadows, and creep, and croak, and fill the ears of the nations with their noisy demonstrations, till they set all the kings and armies of the whole earth in enthusiastic commotion for the final crushing out of the Lamb and all His powers. As in chapter 9, the seven Spirits of God and of Christ went forth into all the earth to make up and gather together into one holy fellowship the great congregation of the sanctified: so these spirits of hell go forth upon the kings and potentates of the world, to make up and gather together the grand army of the Devil's worshippers.[1]

The war rather than *the battle* is a more accurate description of Har Magedon. It is not one decisive battle, but a struggle during the entire last half of the Great Tribulation period. It is precipitated by the king of the north (Ezekiel 38, 39) coming down upon Palestine and is consummated by the coming of Christ (Revelation 19). The crucial moment of the campaign is when the kings of the earth march toward Palestine (see Joel 3:9-16).

Verses 15, 16—Behold, I come as a thief. Blessed is he that watcheth, and keepeth his garments, lest he walk naked, and they see his shame. And he gathered them together into a place called in the Hebrew tongue Armageddon.

Behold, I come as a thief. Blessed is he that watcheth, and keepeth his garments, lest he walk naked, and they see his shame. And he gathered them together into a place which is called in Hebrew Har-Magedon.

Christ does not come to His Church as a thief: "But ye, brethren, are not in darkness, that that day should overtake you as a thief" (I Thes. 5:4). A thief is someone you shut out. Christ does not come as a thief to His Church, for they are looking for Him. However, He does come as a thief to the world at the end of the Great Tribulation (see Revelation 3:3).

[1] J. A. Seiss, *The Apocalypse,* p. 89.

42

But know this, that if the goodman of the house had known in what watch the thief would come, he would have watched, and would not have suffered his house to be broken up (Matt. 24:43).

For yourselves know perfectly that the day of the Lord [not the coming of Christ for His Church but His coming to establish His Kingdom] so cometh as a thief in the night (I Thess. 5:2).

But the day of the Lord will come as a thief in the night; in the which the heavens shall pass away with a great noise, and the elements shall melt with fervent heat, the earth also and the works that are therein shall be burned up (II Peter 3:10).

The attitude for His own during the Great Tribulation, is to watch (see Luke 12:35-40; Matt. 24:42):

Watch ye therefore: for ye know not when the master of the house cometh, at even, or at midnight, or at the cockcrowing, or in the morning (Mark 13:35).

Be sober, be vigilant; because your adversary the devil, as a roaring lion, walketh about, seeking whom he may devour (I Peter 5:8).

Keepeth his garments—Edersheim sheds light on this phrase by explaining that the captain of the temple made his rounds during the night to see if the guards were awake and alert. If any was found asleep, he was either beaten or his garments set on fire.

And they see his shame is literally "they see him not in good form," and reveals that the all important issue, at the return of Christ to set up His kingdom, is watchfulness. At that time His coming will be pinpointed on the prophetic calendar, and faith in Him will be faith in the fact that He will come quickly.

Saints today should have the attitude of waiting rather than watching:

For they themselves show of us what manner of entering in we had unto you, and how ye turned to God from idols to serve the living and true God; and to wait for his Son from heaven, whom he raised from the dead, even Jesus, which delivered us from the wrath to come (I Thess. 1:9, 10).

Looking for that blessed hope, and the glorious appearing of the great God and our Saviour Jesus Christ (Titus 2:13).

Har-Magedon is a war (campaign) and not just a single battle. The last half of the Great Tribulation is the period of this war.

In verse 16 is the only occurrence of the word Har-Magedon in Scripture — though there are many references to it. It means "Mount of Megiddo." It is a compound word made up of the Hebrew "Har," meaning mountain, and "Megiddo," which is a mount in the plain of Esdraelon (Judges 1:27; I Kings 4:12; 9:15; II Kings 9:27). It is a place where many battles have been fought (Judges 5:19 and II Chron. 35:22). It is prophetically dealt with once in the Old Testament (Zech. 12:11). Vincent cites *Clarke's Travels* regarding Megiddo in the plain of Esdraelon:

"... Which has been a chosen place for encampment in every contest carried on in Palestine from the days of Nabuchodonozor king of Assyria, unto the disastrous march of Napoleon Bonaparte from Egypt into Syria. Jews, Gentiles, Saracens, Christian crusaders, and anti-Christian Frenchmen; Egyptians, Persians, Druses, Turks, and

Arabs, warriors of every nation that is under heaven, have pitched their tents on the plain of Esdraelon, and have beheld the banners of their nation wet with the dews of Tabor and Hermon."[1]

Verse 16 gives us the final phase of the war, when Israel will not be able to look for help either to north, east, south or west—since the enemy is coming from all four directions. Help comes from above:

> And I saw heaven opened, and behold a white horse; and he that sat upon him was called Faithful and True, and in righteousness he doth judge and make war (Rev. 19:11).

i. Pouring Out of the SEVENTH BOWL of Wrath, verses 17-21

Verses 17, 18—And the seventh angel poured out his vial into the air and there came a great voice out of the temple of heaven, from the throne, saying, It is done. And there were voices, and thunders, and lightnings; and there was a great earthquake, such as was not since men were upon the earth, so mighty an earthquake, and so great.

And the seventh poured out his bowl upon the air; and a great voice came out of the temple, from the throne, saying, It is done. And there were lightnings, and voices and thunders; and there was a great earthquake, such as was not since there were men upon the earth, so great an earthquake, so mighty.

This is the last series of seven judgments before the coming of Christ and this is the seventh and last of the last seven. We are right at the end of the Great Tribulation here. Let us keep our eyes on Christ through this—He is the judge now.

Upon the air is in space, with no specific geographical location. The Lord Jesus Christ controls space. He is getting ready to come through space.

The Temple has been mentioned with each series of judgments—seals, trumpets, and bowls. However, the temple has been mentioned with the bowls of wrath six times—more than with all the other judgments combined, and this is the last reference to it. There is no temple in the New Jerusalem.

A great voice came out of the temple, from the throne, though it is not identified, I believe it to be the voice of none other than the Son of God. His message is recorded, *It is done.* This is in harmony with His cry upon the cross, "It is finished." At that point in history redemption was wrought and salvation finished for man. There is nothing man can contribute to his salvation; he must simply receive it by faith. For those who have refused God's salvation, there is nothing they can do to escape the judgment of God. It is done. No wonder the writer to the Hebrews wrote:

> How shall we escape, if we neglect so great salvation; which at the first began to be spoken by the Lord, and was confirmed unto us by them that heard him (Heb. 2:3).

Christ is the judge, and the judgment of the Great Tribulation is now concluded. *It is done* is His announcement, and there is nothing ahead but judgment, the Great White Throne of judgment.

Lightnings, voices, and thunders were the solemn announcement, in the beginning of the Great Tribulation, that judgment was impending (see 4:5). They are the final warning of the worst earthquake the world has even witnessed. Ezekiel prophesied of this earthquake:

[1] M. R. Vincent, *Word Studies in the New Testament,* pp. 542, 543

44

So that the fishes of the sea, and the fowls of the heaven, and the beasts of the field, and all creeping things that creep upon the earth, and all the men that are upon the face of the earth, shall shake at my presence, and the mountains shall be thrown down, and the steep places shall fall, and every wall shall fall to the ground (Ezek. 38:20).

Earthquakes are far more destructive than men imagine (see quotations on pages 57 and 58.

Govett makes a sharp distinction in this verse:

The consequences of this bowl, then, appear, first in heaven, then in air, then on earth. First, the voice from the throne; then, angelic voices; then in the air, thunders and lightnings; then the rocking of earth, and its consequences to the abodes of men.[2]

Verses 19-21—And the great city was divided into three parts, and the cities of the nations fell: and great Babylon came in remembrance before God, to give unto her the cup of the wine of the fierceness of his wrath. And every island fled away, and the mountains were not found. And there fell upon men a great hail out of heaven, every stone about the weight of a talent: and men blasphemed God because of the plague of the hail; for the plague thereof was exceeding great.

And the great city became (divided) into three parts, and the cities of the nations fell: and Babylon the great was remembered before God, to give to her the cup of the wine of the indignation of His wrath. And every island fled away, and mountains were not found. And great hail, as it were a talent weight, comes down out of heaven upon men: and men blasphemed God because of the plague of the hail; for the plague thereof is exceeding great.

The great city is Jerusalem which is divided into 3 parts by earthquake. Though the center of the quake is in Jerusalem, it is not confined to Jerusalem.

Cities of the nations fell shows the extent and vast destruction of the earthquake.

Babylon is mentioned specifically again (14:8). The next two chapters give us the details concerning Babylon, and furnish the explanation of the statement, *the cup of the wine of the indignation of His wrath.*

Every island fled away—islands are shifted from one place to another by the earthquake.

Govett suggests that since the article is not used before mountains, all we need supply is *certain* "mountains were not found." (Compare Psalm 18:7, 46:2; Jeremiah 4:24, 26.) Not all, but some of the mountains are removed.

The final act of judgment is the hail storm. The size of the hail stones is enormous—*a talent weight.*

The Greek talent was 56 pounds,
the Jewish talent was 114 pounds.

In Texas we are told of hailstones as big as baseballs. A lady in Iowa has written to say that she could top that—she has seen hail fall in great chunks. Yet most of us have seen how hailstones no bigger than the end of your thumb

[2] Govett, The *Apocalypse Expounded by Scripture*, p. 414

can devastate a corn field or a cotton field. The destruction of hailstones of a talent weight can hardly be imagined. The Roman catapults threw stones this size into Jerusalem, according to the historian Josephus.

There is no place to hide, since the earthquake has shaken down all buildings. This eventuality was predicted by the prophets:

> And the LORD shall cause his glorious voice to be heard, and shall show the lighting down of his arm, with the indignation of his anger, and with the flame of a devouring fire, with scattering, and tempest, and hailstones (Isa. 30:30).

> Say unto them which daub it with untempered morter, that it shall fall: there shall be an overflowing shower; and ye, O great hailstones, shall fall; and a stormy wind shall rend it. . . . Therefore thus saith the Lord God; I will even rend it with a stormy wind in my fury; and there shall be an overflowing shower in mine anger, and great hailstones in my fury to consume it (Ezek. 13:11, 13).

Joshua records the victory of Israel over the kings of the Amorites at Gibeon:

> And it came to pass, as they fled from before Israel, and were in the going down to Bethoron, that the LORD cast down great stones from heaven upon them unto Azekah, and they died: they were more which died with hailstones than they whom the children of Israel slew with the sword (Josh. 10:11).

It would seem that this final and frightening act of judgment would drive men to repentance. Far from it—they increase their blasphemy of God, so adding to their punishment. The heart of man, in its hatred of God, has hardened like concrete. It is difficult for us to accept God's declaration of the human heart as being incurably wicked, yet both history and prophecy confirm it. In order to save some, God had to do a desperate thing. He gave His Son to die! It is necessary for us to let God do some drastic surgery on our stony hearts to make us fit for heaven.

Chapter 17

THEME: The judgment of the Apostate Church in the Great Tribulation; Mystery Babylon; Religion.

OUTLINE:

6. **The Two Babylons Judged,** chapters 17, 18
   a. The **Apostate Church** in the Great Tribulation, chapter 17
      (1). Great **Harlot Riding** the Wild **Beast,** verses 1-7
      (2). Wild **Beast Destroys** the Great **Harlot,** verses 8-18

REMARKS:

So many great issues are brought to a crisis in the Great Tribulation, that it is difficult to keep them separated, and many fine expositors disagree on details. This fact should not be disturbing to believers, as many details will not be clarified until the world enters the Great Tribulation and actually faces the climax to each crisis.

This is especially evident relative to the two Babylons in chapters 17 and 18. Are there *two* Babylons? Are they in two different geographical locations? Are they representative of two different systems? Are they two literal cities or are they the same? The answers to these questions will become clearer as "your redemption draweth nigh." It appears at the present time that two distinct cities are in view.

In chapter 17 it is mystery Babylon—the cosmic church, the apostate church of Thyatira which permitted Jezebel to teach (2:20, 21), which becomes the apostate church of the Great Tribulation (2:22). It has attained the goal of present day apostates of both Romanism, Protestantism and the pagan religions of the world—that of ecumenical ecclesiasticism, one world church. The location of this system is Rome (verse 9). It is called *mystery* Babylon because of its origin. At the tower of Babel man attempted to rally against God. Under Nimrod Babylon became the origin of all false religion.

Hislop has traced this history very carefully and has shown the connection of ancient Babel with modern Rome:

> The Babylonians, in their *popular religion*, supremely worshipped a Goddess Mother and a Son, who was represented in pictures and in images as an infant or child in his mother's arms. . . . From Babylon, this worship of the Mother and the Child spread to the ends of the earth. In Egypt, the Mother and the Child were worshipped under the names of Isis and Osiris. In India, even to this day, as Isi and Iswara; in Asia, as Cybele and Deoius; in Pagan Rome, as Fortuna and Jupiter-puer, or Jupiter, the boy; in Greece, as Ceres, the Great Mother, with the babe at her breast, or as Irene, the goddess of Peace, with the boy Plutus in her arms; and even in Thibet, in China, and Japan, the Jesuit missionaries were astonished to find the counterpart of Madonna and her child as devoutly worshipped as in Papal Rome itself: Shing Moo, the Holy Mother in China, being represented with a child in her arms, and a *glory* around her, exactly as if a Roman Catholic artist had been employed to set her up.
>
> The original of that mother, so widely worshipped, there is reason to believe, was Semiramis, already referred to, who, it is well known,

47

was worshipped by the Babylonians, and other eastern nations, and that under the name of Rhea, the great Goddess "Mother."

It was from the son, however, that she derived all her glory and her claims to deification. That son, though represented as a child in his mother's arms, was a person of great stature and immense bodily powers, as well as most fascinating manners. In Scripture he is referred to (Ezek. viii. 14) under the name of Tammuz, but he is commonly known among classical writers under the name of Bacchus, that is, "The Lamented one." To the ordinary reader the name Bacchus suggests nothing more than revelry and drunkenness, but it is now well known, that amid all the abominations that attended his orgies, their grand design was professedly "the purification of souls," and that from the guilt and defilement of sin. This lamented one, exhibited and adored as a little child in his mother's arms, seems, in point of fact, to have been the *husband* of Semiramis, whose name, Ninus, by which he is commonly known in classical history, literally signified "The Son." As Semiramis, the wife, was worshipped as Rhea, whose grand distinguishing character was that of the great goddess "Mother," the conjunction with her or her husband, under the name of Ninus, or "The Son," was sufficient to originate the peculiar worship of the "Mother and Son," so extensively diffused among the nations of antiquity; and this, no doubt, is the explanation of the fact which has so much puzzled the inquirers into ancient history, that Ninus is sometimes called the *husband*, and sometimes the *son* of Semiramis.[1]

The dream of Nimrod will be realized in the first half of the Great Tribulation when the cosmic church dominates the wild Beast. The church that should have been the bride of Christ is a harlot. She is guilty of spiritual fornication —selling herself to the world for hire. This is the church that says, "I am rich, and increased with goods, and have need of nothing."

This is a pseudo-religious system, which controls the wild Beast in the first half of the Great Tribulation, yet is hated by him. During the last half of the Great Tribulation, the Beast destroys the harlot in order to set up his own religion (see 13:4, 13-15). Dr. Pentecost sums up the end of the harlot system:

> The Beast, who was dominated by the harlot system (Rev. 17:3), rises against her and destroys her and her system completely. Without doubt the harlot system was in competition with the religious worship of the Beast, promoted by the False Prophet, and her destruction is brought about so that the Beast may be the sole object of false worship as he claims to be God.[2]

The Babylon of chapter 18 is a great commercial center and political capital. It is the capital of the Beast. Evidently the Beast rises in Rome, but removes his capital to Babylon. Babylon as a capital was the dream of Alexander the Great, the Caesars, and Napoleon.

Political Babylon, the great commercial center of the world, will be rebuilt. An interesting news item, which may indicate a movement in that direction, appeared in July, 1962:

> According to an announcement of the Ministry of Antiquities in Bagdad, the Tower of Babel is to be rebuilt.

[1] Hislop, *The Two Babylons*, pp. 20-22.
[2] Pentecost, *Things To Come*, p. 368.

48

Although it will not "reach unto heaven," as its original builders intended, it will—nevertheless—provide the tourists with a splendid observation tower more than 300 feet high. From this height, the sight-seers will have a panoramic view of the site of Ancient Babylon.

The reconstruction of the Tower of Babel will be carried out—as far as possible—according to the original dimensions found in ancient documents.

The first tower is supposed to have had a base of nearly 300,000 square feet and had been erected about seventy miles south of Babylon. The re-building of the "Tower of Pride" had been planned already at the time of Alexander the Great. However, this project failed, because the 10,000 workmen required for it, were not available.

After completion of the Tower of Babel, the Iraqi Ministry for Antiquities intends to hold an annual festival, the focal point of which will be the new tower.

That Babylon will be rebuilt in no way contradicts Isaiah 13:19-22, where God states that Babylon will never again be inhabited. Already the ancient site of Babylon is 7 to 9 miles from the Euphrates River. The ancient site is not to be built upon, but a new Babylon, at a new site, will be erected beside the Euphrates River (see author's book, *Initiation Into Isaiah*, chapter 13). However, Isaiah's prophecy could refer to the final destruction, spoken of in Revelation 18, as much of Isaiah deals with the Great Tribulation.

Therefore the wild beasts of the desert with the wild beasts of the islands shall dwell there, and the owls shall dwell therein: and it shall be no more inhabited for ever; neither shall it be dwelt in from generation to generation. As God overthrew Sodom and Gomorrah and the neighbour cities thereof, saith the LORD; so shall no man abide there, neither shall any son of man dwell therein (Jer. 50:39, 40).

Babylon is suddenly fallen and destroyed: howl for her; take balm for her pain, if so be she may be healed. . . . Behold, I am against thee, O destroying mountain, saith the LORD, which destroyest all the earth: and I will stretch out mine hand upon thee, and roll thee down from the rocks, and will make thee a burnt mountain. And they shall not take of thee a stone for a corner, nor a stone for foundations; but thou shalt be desolate for ever, saith the LORD (Jer. 51:8, 25, 26).

Jeremiah is looking forward to the destruction described in Revelation 18: 21-23.

Ecclesiastical Babylon is destroyed by the wild Beast.

Commercial Babylon is destroyed by the Return of Christ.

Ecclesiastical Babylon is hated by the Beast (17:16).

Commercial Babylon is loved by the world (18:9, 19).

Ecclesiastical Babylon is destroyed at the beginning of the last $3\frac{1}{2}$ years of the Great Tribulation (17:15-18).

Commercial Babylon is destroyed at the end of the last $3\frac{1}{2}$ years of the Great Tribulation (18:8; 19:11-16).

Zechariah 5:5-11 is interesting in this connection, and sheds much light upon the shift of political power to Babylon, and the relocation of the commercial center of the world.

Finally, this 17th chapter of Revelation reveals the most frightful, terrifying, dreadful, and awe-inspiring vision in the Scriptures.

Babylon, religious, commercial, and political is Satan's capital of the world. Babylon is mentioned in the Bible more than any other city, with the exception of Jerusalem—and it is older than Jerusalem. It is the second oldest city mentioned in the Bible (Enoch is the oldest, Gen. 4:17).

COMMENT:

   a. The **Apostate Church** in the Great Tribulation, chapter 17
   (1). Great **Harlot Riding** the Wild **Beast,** verses 1-7

Verses 1, 2—And there came one of the seven angels which had the seven vials, and talked with me, saying unto me, Come hither; I will show unto thee the judgment of the great whore that sitteth upon many waters: with whom the kings of the earth have committed fornication, and the inhabitants of the earth have been made drunk with the wine of her fornication.

And there came one of the (7) seven angels that had the (7) seven bowls, and spake with me, saying, Come hither, I will show thee the judgment of the great harlot that sitteth upon many waters; with whom the kings of the earth committed fornication, and they that dwell in the earth were made drunken with the wine of her fornication.

One of the seven angels that had the seven bowls closely identifies this final judgment of God on Babylon with the seven bowls of wrath. For this reason we do not agree that a new series of seven judgments is initiated here; but rather the seven bowls of wrath are the final judgments of God, which come to a crisis at Babylon. The destruction of commercial Babylon means that the kingdom of the wild Beast is broken.

The great harlot is an expressive and vivid description of religious defection, and is altogether scriptural. Hosea bases his entire message on his own private life when he married a harlot who proved to be unfaithful to him. He likens this to God's relationship to the nation of Israel, as Israel played the harlot by lapsing into idolatry. (see author's booklet, *The Greatest Sin In All the World*, also read Hosea 1 and 2; Isa. 1:21; Jer. 2:20; 3:1, 2, 6, 8, 9; Ezek. 16:15, 16, 28, 31, 35, 41; 23:5, 19, 44.

The church of Thyatira only permitted Jezebel to teach (2:20), but the apostate church of the Great Tribulation is a harlot more frightful than was Jezebel. It is that part of the church that will remain after the true Church has been raptured. It will be composed of those who have never trusted Christ as Saviour, who do not love Him and do not know Him. However, it will not be confined to this group, but will be an amalgamation of all cults and all pagan religions. You don't think you could have a world religion without including Buddhism and Mohammedanism, do you? This is ecumenical ecclesiasticism with a vengeance, and to the nth degree. At the present time there is a definite drive to bring together the different fragmentations of Christendom. The titular head of the Church of England, Archbishop Geoffrey F. Fisher, is visiting the pope in Rome. The National Council of Churches, meeting in San Francisco, drives toward unity in a new upsurge of interest. The Reverend Mr.

Max Lackmann, a German Lutheran theologian, said in Rome recently that the time has come for groups of Lutherans to join the Roman Catholic church. The pope has called for a council on unity. Even some evangelicals talk about sitting down at the council table with Roman Catholics in order that a better understanding might be established. We wonder if the apostle John would have been so "broadminded" with Celsus, or Luther with the pope.

This world church will boost the Antichrist to power. But the Antichrist will get rid of the church in time, because it does worship God, and he wants for himself the sole worship of man.

That sitteth upon many waters. The many waters represent great masses of people, and the thought here is that this great satanic religious system dominates multitudes of the world's population for a brief time (verse 15).

Kings of the earth committed fornication shows definitely that church and state are joined together in an unholy alliance. The rulers use the apostate church to control the masses; and the church yields to this arrangement for political preferment and power. We are seeing the beginning of this, and it is a much greater danger to America than is communism.

Such a power-bloc dazzles the unthinking mob and they come under the influence of the wild Beast out of the sea and the wild Beast out of the earth. They are made religious alcoholics. When you reject the genuine, you are wide open for the spurious. It is worthy to note that in our day false cults do not pioneer, but they follow where the truth has penetrated, they leave a slimy trail wherever the gospel has gone. So here those who drink the wine of her fornication have declined the cup of salvation, and there is pressed to their lips that which makes them drunk.

Verses 3-5—So he carried me away in the spirit into the wilderness: and I saw a woman sit upon a scarlet coloured beast, full of names of blasphemy, having seven heads and ten horns. And the woman was arrayed in purple and scarlet colour, and decked with gold and precious stones and pearls, having a golden cup in her hand full of abominations and filthiness of her fornication: and upon her forehead was a name written, MYSTERY, BABYLON THE GREAT, THE MOTHER OF HARLOTS AND ABOMINATIONS OF THE EARTH.

And he carried me away in the Spirit into a wilderness; and I saw a woman sitting upon a scarlet-colored wild beast, full of names of blasphemy, having seven heads and ten horns. And the woman was clothed in purple and scarlet, and gilded with gold, and precious stone and pearls, having in her hand a golden cup full of abominations, even the unclean things of her fornication, and upon her forehead a name writter MYSTERY, BABYLON THE GREAT, THE MOTHER OF THE HARLOTS AND OF THE ABOMINATIONS OF THE EARTH.

Two factors enter into this vision which we have not seen heretofore: 1) John is carried away in the Spirit, 2) into a wilderness. Remember that John was on the Isle of Patmos in the Spirit for the vision of the glorified Christ and His message to the churches. At that time John was caught up to heaven. From then on the scene shifts from heaven to earth. However, here we are told again that John was in the Spirit. Did he need a fresh anointing of the Spirit for this vision? Is the wilderness literal? Remember this chapter is a vision where symbols are used. Around both Babylon and Rome is a literal wilderness, which is a matter of recorded history. Babylon was to become a wilderness. In this connection read Isaiah 47, 48 and Jeremiah 50, 51. Outside of Rome the wilderness is called the campagna. We believe that the wilderness mentioned in this verse is literal; but also that it is a sign of the chaotic condition of the world brought about by the religious confusion of Babylon.

John saw a *woman sitting upon a scarlet colored wild beast.* The wild Beast has previously been identified—the Antichrist ruling over the restored Roman Empire. The woman is identified for us in verse 18. The woman is a city and the city is Rome, the religious capital of the world, which has inherited all the false religion and satanic system of ancient Babylon. That the city is Rome is further clarified by verse 9. Rome was the city set on seven hills—known as such to both pagan and Christian writers. Horace wrote, "The gods, who look with favour on the seven hills . . ." Ovid added, "But Rome looks around on the whole globe from her seven mountains, the seat of empire and abode of the gods." Augustine wrote, "Babylon is a former Rome, and Rome is a later·Babylon." In these verses the city of Rome is assuredly in view. The woman, the harlot representing the religious system dominates the Roman Empire at the beginning of the Great Tribulation.

Full of names of blasphemy shows how far religion had departed from the living God.

Clothed in purple and scarlet. Purple was the predominant color of Roman imperialism. Every senator and knight wore a purple stripe as a badge of his position, and the emperor's robes were purple. *Scarlet* is the color adopted by Roman Catholicism. Popes and cardinals are clothed in scarlet.

Gilded with gold shows the beauty of the outward display, but like the Pharisees, it is within "full of dead men's bones and of all uncleanness."

Precious stone and pearls are pretty cold, though they may be genuine, and are a sordid imitation of genuine heart-felt religion:

> Woe unto you. scribes and Pharisees, hypocrites! for ye make clean the outside of the cup and of the platter, but within they are full of extortion and excess (Matt. 23:25).

This boastful display without taste reveals the material wealth of the apostate church (see Revelation 3:17).

A golden cup full of abominations is the religious intoxication of the antichurch (not Antichrist) and a pseudo-religion, counterfeit Christianity, a fake and false gospel, and a sham and spurious system. This is the cup which makes the world drunk:

> Babylon hath been a golden cup in the LORD'S hand, that made all the earth drunken: the nations have drunken of her wine; therefore the nations are mad (Jer. 51:7).

It is a toast to "the lie" because the drink is "strong delusion."

Upon her forehead a name written is a startling revelation of the character of the woman. She does not wear a crown but rather the mark of her ancient profession. Vincent gives us this clarifying statement:

As was customary with harlots, who had their names inscribed on a ticket. Seneca, addressing a wanton priestess, "Nomen tuum pependit a fronte," *thy name hung from thy forehead*. See Juvenal, Satire vi., 123 sqq., of the profligate Messalina, "having falsely assumed the ticket of Lycisca."

MYSTERY BABYLON THE GREAT, THE MOTHER OF HARLOTS AND OF THE ABOMINATIONS OF THE EARTH is the repugnant label and odious badge for the church. Notice that the Church that belonged to Christ is a bride, this church is a harlot.

The true Church is a mystery in that it was not revealed in the Old Testament (see Ephesians 3:1-9). The anti-church is a mystery in that it was not revealed until John wrote Revelation 17. At that time all the other apostles were dead. Paul had written of "the mystery of iniquity":

For the mystery of iniquity doth already work: only he who now hinders will hinder until he be taken out of the way (II Thess. 2:7).

The anti-church is the antithesis of the true Church, which is the virgin Bride of Christ, and it is the consummation of the working of "the mystery of iniquity."

It is *mystery Babylon* because it is given this designation, as Jerusalem is called Sodom (see Revelation 11:8 and Isaiah 1:9, 10).

Babylon is the fountainhead for all false religion, therefore she is *the mother of the harlots and of the abominations of the earth*. This is by far Scripture's most expressive and vivid picture of awful and abominable sin. Sex and false religions are related.

Verses 6, 7—And I saw the woman drunken with the blood of the saints, and with the blood of the martyrs of Jesus: and when I saw her, I wondered with great admiration. And the angel said unto me, Wherefore didst thou marvel? I will tell thee the mystery of the woman, and of the beast that carrieth her, which hath the seven heads and ten horns.

And I saw the woman drunken with the blood of the saints, and with the blood of the martyrs of Jesus. And when I saw her, I wondered with a great wonder. And the angel said unto me, Wherefore didst thou wonder? I will tell thee the mystery of the woman, and of the wild beast that is carrying her, which hath the seven heads and ten horns.

The harlot not only makes others drunk, but she is intoxicated by her acts of persecution.

The saints refer to Old Testament saints.

Martyrs of Jesus refer to New Testament saints.

This indicates that Babylon is more than Roman Catholicism. It is an amalgam of all religions. All the true believers were caught up at the Rapture. Babylon is the residue of what is left; it is a composite church which includes both Roman Catholic, Protestant and all other religions. It is confusion compounded and is the fountainhead of all religious error and idolatry. Babylon in the Old Testament persecuted God's people and was the enemy of God. It was Babylon that put the Hebrew children in the fiery furnace because they would not worship an image.

[1] Vincent, *Word Studies in the New Testament*, p. 544.

John marveled at the harlot because this was something new to him. The angel asks John why he should wonder, when he was present to explain the mystery of the woman.

John is here emphasizing the Roman Empire aspect of the wild Beast rather than the Antichrist aspect.

(2). Wild **Beast Destroys** the Great **Harlot**, verses 8-18

Verses 8-10—The beast that thou sawest was, and is not; and shall ascend out of the bottomless pit, and go into perdition: and they that dwell on the earth shall wonder, whose names were not written in the book of life from the foundation of the world, when they behold the beast that was, and is not, and yet is. And here is the mind which hath wisdom. The seven heads are seven mountains, on which the woman sitteth. And there are seven kings: five are fallen, and one is, and the other is not yet come; and when he cometh, he must continue a short space.

The wild beast which thou sawest was and is not; and is about to come up out of the abyss, and to go (goeth) into perdition. And those dwelling on the earth shall wonder, whose names are not written upon the book of life from the foundation of the world (cosmos), when they behold the wild beast because it was, and is not, and shall come (be present). Here is the mind having wisdom. The seven heads are seven mountains on which the woman sitteth. And there are seven kings; the five have fallen (fell), the one is, the other is not yet come; and when he cometh, he must continue a little while.

The wild Beast *was* speaks of the past history of the Roman Empire. *Is not* refers to the present condition of the fragmented Empire. *Is about to come up out of the abyss* speaks of the reactivation of the Roman Empire by Satan (Rev. 13:1).

To go (goeth) into perdition speaks of the destruction of the Roman Empire by the Coming of Christ. The reappearance of the Roman Empire in its great power will win the admiration of the peoples of the world who are not redeemed. They will respect and worship the Antichrist for his brilliant *coup d'etat.* God's saints will have the mind of the Spirit and will understand and not be spiritually stupid:

> But ye have an unction from the Holy One, and ye know all things . . . .But the anointing which ye have received of him abideth in you, and ye need not that any man teach you: but as the same anointing teacheth you all things, and is truth, and is no lie, and even as it hath taught you, ye shall abide in him (I John 2:20, 27).

And there are seven kings is taken by some (including Newell and Govett) to mean individual rulers.

Five have fallen (fell)—Govett gives the following list:

(1) Julius Caesar — assassinated

(2) Tiberius — Poisoned or smothered

(3) Caligula — assassinated

(4) Claudius — poisoned

(5) Nero — committed suicide

The one is refers to Domitian who was living in John's day—who also was assassinated.

The other is yet to come refers to Antichrist. Other expositors (as Scofield and Walter Scott) consider these seven as the different forms of government through which Rome passed. These are listed as Kings, Consuls, Dictators, Decemvirs, and Military Tribunes. *The one is* refers to the 6th or imperial form of government set up by Julius Caesar, and under which John was banished by Domitian. The seventh and last, though it has not yet appeared, will be satanic in form.

Regardless of the interpretation adopted, the end in view is the same—the Antichrist rules over the reactivated Roman Empire.

Verses 11-14—And the beast that was, and is not, even he is the eighth, and is of the seven, and goeth into perdition. And the ten horns which thou sawest are ten kings, which have received no kingdom as yet; but receive power as kings one hour with the beast. These have one mind, and shall give their power and strength unto the beast. These shall make war with the Lamb, and the Lamb shall overcome them: for he is Lord of lords, and King of kings: and they that are with him are called, and chosen, and faithful.

And the beast that was, and is not, is himself also an eighth, and is of the seven, and is going into perdition. And the two horns that thou sawest are ten kings, who (of the kind which) have received no kingdom as yet; but they receive authority as kings, with the wild beast, for one hour. These have one mind, and they give (over) their power and authority unto the beast. These shall war with the Lamb, and the Lamb shall overcome them, for He is Lord of lords, and King of kings; and those with Him (shall overcome), called and chosen and faithful.

Govett comments, "At times the Wild Beast signifies, *generally, the Roman empire.* . . . But it signifies also the last or eighth head; that is, the individual emperor who is Antichrist." [1]

Here the Antichrist is designated. He is the "little horn" of Daniel who puts down three horns (kings) when he comes to power (see Daniel 7:8, 24 and author's book, *Delving Through Daniel,* also the comment on Revelation 13:3).

The beast that was refers to the past history of the Roman Empire under the emperors.

And is not refers to the end of Imperial Rome with its global empire, which came to an end during the 3rd to the 5th century (the exact date is unimportant), and is in fragments today.

Is himself also an eighth, but is of the seven identifies the Antichrist with the return to the imperial form of the restored Roman Empire. He is the "little horn" of Daniel chapter 7. He is not one of the 10 horns, but is separate from them. He is an eighth head in this seven, yet he is one of the seven since he restores the last form of government to Rome.

And is going into perdition is the constant reference to final judgment of the Antichrist (see Rev. 19:20; 20:10), the lake of fire.

The ten horns are the same as the ten horns of Daniel 7:7. These ten kings will reign with the Antichrist, but will be subservient to him. They willingly or unwillingly give over their authority to the Antichrist and become his puppets.

[1] Govett, *The Apocalypse Expounded by Scripture,* pp. 447, 448.

The Antichrist is opposed to Christ and is His enemy. This antagonist will make a supreme and last attempt to dethrone Christ. The effort is insane, eventuating in the defeat of Antichrist.

During the Great Tribulation the elect were forbidden to oppose Antichrist, but now they are permitted to join with Christ in His victory over Antichrist.

Verses 15-18—And he saith unto me, The waters which thou sawest, where the whore sitteth, are peoples, and multitudes, and nations, and tongues. And the ten horns which thou sawest upon the beast, these shall hate the whore, and shall make her desolate and naked, and shall eat her flesh, and burn her with fire. For God hath put in their hearts to fulfil his will, and to agree, and give their kingdom unto the beast, until the words of God shall be fulfilled. And the woman which thou sawest is that great city, which reigneth over the kings of the earth.

And he saith to me, The waters which thou sawest where the harlot sitteth, are peoples, and multitudes (mobs), and nations, and tongues. And the ten horns which thou sawest, and the beast, these shall hate the harlot, and shall make her desolated and naked, and shall eat her flesh, and shall burn her (down) with fire. For God did put into their hearts to do His mind, and to come to one mind, and to give their kingdom unto the beast, until the words of God shall be fulfilled. And the woman whom thou sawest is the great city, which hath a kingdom over the kings of the earth.

The waters are explained to be the many ethnological groups as well as the nations of the world. This figure is in harmony with that used in the Old Testament (see Isa. 8:7; Psalm 18:4, 16; 124). The position of the harlot reveals that she is ruling over them for but a brief time.

The *ten horns* are ten kings (verse 12) who rule over the different divisions of the Roman Empire. They in turn give over to the Beast their kingdoms which solidifies the Roman Emipre, and enables the Beast to lift himself up as a world dictator.

For a time the Beast (Antichrist) is willing to share his place of exaltation with the harlot, since she has also sought to advance his cause while dividing his glory. This he hates, and the ten kings are one with him in this. The Antichrist not only breaks his covenant with Israel, but he also breaks his relationship with the apostate church. This hatred against the apostate church is so violent that the reaction is described as the cannibalistic picking of her bones, then burning them with fire.

In this, the Antichrist and his 10 allies are fulfilling the Word of God and carrying out His will as did the Assyrian, as predicted in Isaiah 10:5-19, and as did Caesar Augustus in Luke 2:1-7.

By eliminating the apostate church, the way is cleared for the worship of Antichrist, as advocated by the false prophet (see Revelation 13:14-18).

The *woman* is further identified as a city, the city of Rome (see verse 9).

This is the frightful but just end of the apostate church. However, it does not improve the situation, but rather introduces the darkest period for religion in the history of the world. The reign and religion of Antichrist is the darkest hour earth has known—yet is the inevitable end of the distrust which began in the Garden of Eden, was given a new impetus at the Tower of Babel, and finally crucified Jesus Christ. Having rejected the truth, the only alternative was to believe the big lie, the strong delusion. It culminates in the catastrophic Coming of Christ. This is the just retribution of error and evil.

Chapter 18

THEME: Judgment of commercial Babylon; reaction of earth and heaven.

OUTLINE:

b. **Political and Commercial Babylon Judged,** chapter 18

(1). **Announcement** of Fall of Commercial and Political Babylon,
verses 1-8

(2). **Anguish** in the World Because of Judgment on Babylon, verses 9-19

(3). **Anticipation** of Joy in Heaven Because of Judgment of Babylon,
verses 20-24

REMARKS:

In chapters 17 and 18 two Babylons are brought before us. The Babylon of chapter 17 is ecclesiastical. The Babylon of chapter 18 is economic. The first is religious—the apostate church. The second is political and commercial. The apostate church is hated by the kings of the earth (Rev. 17:16); the commercial center is loved by the kings of the earth (Rev. 18:9). The apostate church is destroyed by the kings of the earth; political Babylon is destroyed by the judgment of God (verses 5, 8). Obviously, mystery Babylon is destroyed first—in the midst of the Great Tribulation; while commercial Babylon is destroyed at the Second Coming of Christ. These two Babylons are not one and the same city. Mystery Babylon is Rome; commercial Babylon is ancient Babylon, rebuilt as the commercial capital of the world. This city is the final capital of the political power of the Beast (see Zech. 5:5-11).

There is no unanimous consent on the part of conservative expositors that ancient Babylon will be rebuilt. The passage in Isaiah 13:19-22 does not preclude the possibility of the rebuilding of ancient Babylon, provided it is interpreted as the fulfillment of the final destruction of Babylon in Revelation 18. However, in view of the fact that the Euphrates River, on which ancient Babylon was situated, has shifted its course, makes it highly unlikely that the exact site will be the location of the city. Its ancient prestige and favorable location as a great global center for commerce, makes the rebuilding of Babylon a reasonable conclusion. Also its easy accessibility to both East and West makes it a strategic political capital.

Govett calls attention to the absence of any reference to the horns and heads of the Beast in this chapter. Hence he concludes that this is literal Babylon.

There are two views of the destruction of Babylon which are diametrically opposed to each other. The viewpoint and perspective are highly important. (1) The reaction of men of business and politics is one of great anguish. To them it is the depth of tragedy. It means the total bankruptcy of big business. (2) The second reaction is that of heaven. It is one of joy that the holiness and justice of God is vindicated. It means the end of man's sinful career on earth.

COMMENT:

(1). **ANNOUNCEMENT OF FALL** of Commercial and Political Babylon,
verses 1-8

Verse 1—And after these things I saw another angel come down from heaven, having great power; and the earth was lightened with his glory.

After these things I saw another angel coming down out of heaven, having great authority; and the earth was lightened with his glory.

Here again is the interesting statement, *after these things* (meta tauta). After what things? After the series of 7's, after the judgment of religious Babylon come these things. We are still in the last major division of this book.

I saw—John is still a spectator.

Another angel takes us back to chapter 14 where a series of six angels are mentioned with the sole identification of "another angel." He is a divine supernatural messenger of God, but faceless and nameless.

With great authority indicates that this angel has a superior rank to the other "another angels" and has brought an important message.

And the earth was lightened with his glory further signifies the prestige of this angel (Ezek. 43:2).

Verse 2—And he cried mightily with a strong voice, saying, Babylon the great is fallen, is fallen, and is become the habitation of devils, and the hold of every foul spirit, and a cage of every unclean and hateful bird.

And he shouted with a mighty voice, saying, Fell, fell is Babylon the great, and became a habitation of demons, and a prison (hold, cage) of every unclean spirit, and a prison (hold, cage) of every unclean and hated bird.

The preliminary announcement of the fall of Babylon was made in 14:8. The angel here is greater in authority than the one who made the first announcement.

Fell, fell is Babylon, and became are in the Greek prophetic aorist, which speaks of coming events as if they have already transpired. In God's plan and program it is just as though it had already taken place. He knows the end from the beginning.

A habitation of demons, and a prison (hold, cage) of every unclean spirit, and a prison (hold, cage) of every unclean and hated bird indicates that this is where demons of the spirit world and unclean birds of the physical world will be incarcerated during the Millennium. Isaiah and Jeremiah confirm this (Isa. 13:19-22 and Jer. 50:38-40). Does this not show that the prophecies of both Isaiah and Jeremiah find a final fulfillment in the destruction of literal Babylon of Revelation 18? If this is true, then there is no prophecy which forbids Babylon from being rebuilt. Babylon is the headquarters of demons, and has been the place of rebellion through the years.

Verse 3—For all nations have drunk of the wine of the wrath of her fornication, and the kings of the earth have committed fornication with her, and the merchants of the earth are waxed rich through the abundance of her delicacies.

For by the wine of the wrath of her fornication all the nations have drunk (or are fallen); and the kings of the earth committed fornication with her, and the merchants of the earth waxed rich by the power of her wantonness.

Have drunk (or are fallen) are the two permitted renderings which have good manuscript authority. Both are true. The normal rendering is *have drunk*, but this is God's judgment on "big business" which denies God's authority. This is the unholy alliance of government and business.

The word for merchants means those who travel. It is not those who produce goods or manufacture goods, but those who are brokers, engaging in business for a big profit. Business is a sacred cow that nothing must harm or hinder. Men use business as the biggest excuse for having no time for God, yet these same men must finally stand before God. God will judge godless commercialism.

Verse 4—And I heard another voice from heaven, saying, Come out of her, my people, that ye be not partakers of her sins, and that ye receive not of her plagues.

And I heard another voice out of heaven, saying, Come forth out of her, my people, that ye have no fellowship with her sins, and that ye received not of her plagues.

The one who is speaking here is none other than the Son of God, and He is calling His people out of Babylon before the judgment comes. It is a physical separation with a corollary in the experience of Lot in Sodom. As Lot was warned to get out of Sodom to escape the deluge of fire (Gen. 19), these people of God are warned (see Deut. 4:30, 31). Such was also God's warning to Israel (see Jer. 51:5, 6, 45 and Isa. 48:20). The warning is two fold: (1) they are to have no fellowship with the sins of Babylon; (2) and they are to flee before judgment falls.

This has a pertinent application for us today. It should be a warning to us— not that God will not save His own from this hour, but He wants us to be separate, not indulging the old nature, but walking by the Spirit. If we will not deal with sin here and now by confessing and forsaking it, He will deal with it. Either He will judge it now or it will meet us at the judgment seat of Christ. God gives us the opportunity of judging our sin today:

> For if we would judge ourselves, we should not be judged. But when we are judged, we are chastened of the Lord, that we should not be condemned with the world (I Cor. 11:31, 32).

How can we judge our own sin? I John 1:9 has the answer. We are to confess it (confess means to say the same thing that God says about it, take God's viewpoint of it—"God, I agree with You about this thing"). But if we refuse to judge ourselves, God will judge us. The sin of some folk will not be settled until the judgment seat of Christ. I hope to get all my accounts straightened out down here. Because God may not take us to the woodshed immediately does not mean that He is letting us get by with sin. No one is getting by, judgment is coming.

Verse 5—For her sins have reached unto heaven, and God hath remembered her iniquities.

Babylon has a long history of accumulated sins, and God has the record. Finally judgment breaks like a flood upon this city and system. The judgment of God may be delayed, but it is sure. It may seem to us that the unbeliever is getting by with sin, but God's judgment is coming.

Verse 6—Reward her even as she rewarded you, and double unto her double according to her works: in the cup which she hath filled fill to her double.

Render unto her even as she also rendered, and double unto her the double according to her works; in the cup which she mingled, mingle unto her double

This is poetic justice (see Obadiah 15). The cup of iniquity is being filled to the brim; when the last drop is poured in, it is pressed to the lips of those who committed iniquity. This is just (see Psalm 137).

Verse 7—How much she hath glorified herself, and lived deliciously, so much torment and sorrow give her: for she saith in her heart, I sit a queen, and am no widow, and shall see no sorrow.

How much soever she glorified herself, and waxed wanton (lived in luxury), so much give her of torment and mourning; for she saith in her heart, I sit a queen, and am no widow, and shall in no wise see mourning.

The prosperity of Babylon blinded her to the judgment of God. Trading was active on the stock market and everyone bought blue chip issues right up to the moment of judgment. Luxury, arrogance, pride, and self-deception characterized the spirit of this godless city. World peace was in sight, and optimism was the spirit of the day. Only the prophets of gloom issued a warning, and they were classified as "squares," as was Noah.

Verse 8—Therefore shall her plagues come in one day, death, and mourning, and famine; and she shall be utterly burned with fire: for strong is the Lord God who judgeth her.

Therefore in one day shall her plagues come, death, and mourning, and famine; and she shall utterly be burned up with fire; for strong is the Lord God who judged her.

This calls to our attention the suddenness of destruction and that it will be by *fire.*

So great is her grief that *mourning* is counted a plague along with *death* and *famine.* Death, mourning, and famine are the three horsemen who ride roughshod over Babylon. The destruction is total and final. In the Scriptures this is the first city of prominence, but its long, eventful, and sinful history ends.

Strong is the Lord God who judged her— it is God who destroys this city, because He alone is able to do so. He does so, we believe, at the Return of Christ to the earth:

Who is this that cometh from Edom, with dyed garments from Bozrah? this that is glorious in his apparel, travelling in the greatness of his strength? I that speak in righteousness, mighty to save. Wherefore art thou red in thine apparel, and thy garments like him that treadeth in the winefat? I have trodden the wineprsss alone; and of the people there was none with me: for I will tread them in mine anger, and trample them in my fury; and their blood shall be sprinkled upon my garments, and I will stain all my raiment. For the day of vengeance is in mine heart, and the year of my redeemed is come(Isa. 63:1-4).

In His second coming Christ is seen coming from Edom with blood sprinkled garments—I believe He has come by Babylon and has executed judgment on that wicked city. See also Revelation 19:1-13.

(2). **ANGUISH IN THE WORLD** Because of Judgment on Babylon,
verses 9-19

Verses 9, 10—And the kings of the earth, who have committed fornication and lived deliciously with her, shall bewail her, and lament for her, when they shall see the smoke of her burning, standing afar off for the fear of her torment, saying, Alas, alas, that great city Babylon, that mighty city! for in one hour is thy judgment come.

And the kings of the earth, who committed fornication and lived deliciously (in luxury) with her, shall weep and wail over her, when they look upon the smoke of her burning, standing afar off for the fear of her torment, saying, Woe, woe, the great city, Babylon, the strong city! for in one hour is thy judgment come.

In this day Babylon will dominate and rule the world, she will have the first total dictatorship. The stock market will be read from Babylon; Babylon will set the styles for the world; a play to be successful will have to be a success in Babylon. And everything in the city is in rebellion against Almighty God and centers in Antichrist. No one dreamed that this great city would be judged. Yet by the time the sun went down, Babylon was nothing but smoldering ruins. When the news goes out the world is stunned, and then begins the wail. The whole world will howl when Babylon goes down. You will have to tune down your earphones if you are on the moon.

We saw in chapter 17 that the kings of the earth hated religious Babylon and destroyed her; but here in chapter 18 we see that the kings of the earth love commercial Babylon because of the revenue she brought to their coffers. This is an unholy alliance of politics and big business. They desert Babylon like rats leaving a sinking ship; their mourning is both pathetic and contemptible. They eulogize her with panegyrics of praise, but there is a hopelessness in their anguish. They marvel at the sudden destruction of that which they thought was gilt-edged security. The judgment came in the space of one hour, reminding us of the sudden devastation caused by atomic explosions.

Verses 11-17a—And the merchants of the earth shall weep and mourn over her; for no man buyeth their merchandise any more: the merchandise of gold, and silver, and precious stones, and of pearls, and fine linen, and purple, and silk, and scarlet, and all thyine wood, and all manner vessels of ivory, and all manner vessels of most precious wood, and of brass, and iron, and marble, and cinnamon, and odours, and ointments, and frankincense, and wine, and oil, and fine flour, and wheat, and beasts, and sheep, and horses, and chariots, and slaves, and souls of men. And the fruits that thy soul lusted after are departed from thee, and all things which were dainty and goodly are departed from thee, and thou shalt find them no more at all. The merchants of these things, which were made rich by her, shall stand afar off for the fear of her torment, weeping and wailing, and saying, Alas, alas, that great city, that was clothed in fine linen, and purple, and scarlet, and decked with gold, and precious stones, and pearls! For in one hour so great riches is come to nought.

Everything listed here is a luxury item. Babylon will make these luxury items necessities. You will not find a cotton dress or a pair of overalls anywhere in this list.

And the merchants of the earth weep and mourn over her, for no man buyeth their merchandise (cargo) any more: merchandise (cargo) of gold, and silver, and precious stones, and pearls,

Then we move from the jewelry department to the ladies' ready-to-wear:

. . . *and fine linen, and purple, and silk, and scarlet;*

Then to the luxury gift department:

. . . *and all thyine (citron) wood, and every vessel of ivory, and every vessel made of most precious wood, and of brass, and iron, and marble;*

We move on to the spice and cosmetic department:

. . . *and cinnamon, and spice (amomum), and odours, and ointment, and frankincense,*

To the liquor department and the pastry center:

. . . *and wine, and oil, and fine flour, and wheat* [this is the food of the rich, see 6:6, barley was the food of the poor]

On to the meat department for T-bone steaks and lamb chops:

. . . *and cattle, and sheep,*

The merchandise covers every phase of business. The articles are for a society accustomed to the better things of the material universe. Even men were bought and sold—including their souls.

. . . *and merchandise of horses, and chariots, and slaves (bodies), and souls of men.*

The merchants of these things who grew rich by her, shall stand afar off because of the fear of her torment, saying, Alas, alas (ouai, ouai) for the great city. Alas is a very weak translation of the cry, *Ouai.* The very sound of the word *ouai* is a form of wailing. The merchants of the earth sit before their T.V. screens and cry, "Ouai, ouai," for in one hour wealth so great was laid desolate.

We always have been able to find a parallel in the Old Testament. Do we have anything that corresponds to this in the past? Yes, Ezekiel predicted the judgment of Tyre, the capital of the Phoenicians. Tyre was to the ancient world what New York City is today and Babylon is to the future. See Ezekiel 26 and 27.

Verses 17b-19—And every shipmaster, and all the company in ships, and sailors, and as many as trade by sea, stood afar off, and cried when they saw the smoke of her burning, saying, What city is like unto this great city! And they cast dust on their heads, and cried, weeping and wailing, saying, Alas, alas, that great city, wherein were made rich all that had ships in the sea by reason of her costliness! for in one hour is she made desolate.

And every shipmaster and every one that sails anywhere (traveler) and sailors, and those who live by seafaring stood afar off. And cried out when they looked upon the smoke of her burning, saying, What city is like the great city? And they cast dust upon their heads, and cried, weeping and mourning, saying, Woe, woe (ouai, ouai), the great city wherein all that had their ships in the sea were made rich by reason of her costly expenditure! for in one hour is she made desolate.

The third delegation of mourners is composed of those engaged in transportation—the great public carriers. They had become rich by transporting the merchandise of Babylon. Now there is no more business. They mourn because of the depression. All went up in smoke in a moment. They, like the others, marvel at the sudden destruction.

All of this has an application for us. How do we see the luxury of this world? Do we see it as it really is? Can we use it without getting it into our hearts? How would you feel if the luxuries in your life, which you have come to consider necessities, suddenly went up in smoke? Would it break your heart, or is your heart in heaven, fixed on Christ?

(3). ANTICIPATION OF JOY IN HEAVEN Because of Judgment of Babylon, verses 20-24

Verse 20—Rejoice over her, thou heaven, and ye holy apostles and prophets; for God hath avenged you on her.

Rejoice over her, thou heaven, and ye saints, and ye apostles, and ye prophets; for God hath judged your judgment on her.

The viewpoint of heaven is entirely different. It is no funeral procession there. Rather it is the celebration of an anticipated event. The saints prayed for it; the prophets of the Old Testament and the apostles of the New Testament predicted it. Now all is fulfilled and there is joy, for God has exonerated His name.

Verse 21—And a mighty angel took up a stone like a great millstone, and cast it into the sea, saying, Thus with violence shall that great city Babylon be thrown down, and shall be found no more at all.

And one strong angel took up a stone like a great millstone, and cast it into the sea, saying, Thus with a mighty rush (fall) shall Babylon, the mighty city, be cast down, and shall be found no more at all.

Even heaven calls our attention to the violence, suddenness, and complete annihilation of Babylon. Like a stone that makes a big splash and then disappears beneath the waves will Babylon come to an end.

Verses 22, 23—And the voice of harpers, and musicians, and of pipers, and trumpeters, shall be heard no more at all in these; and no craftsman, of whatsoever craft he be, shall be found any more in thee; and the sound of a millstone shall be heard no more at all in thee; and the light of a candle shall shine no more at all in thee; and the voice of the bridegroom and of the bride shall be heard no more at all in thee: for thy merchants were the great men of the earth; for by thy sorceries were all nations deceived.

And the voice of harpers and minstrels and flute-players and trumpeters shall be heard no more at all in thee; and no more craftsman, of whatsoever craft shall be found any more at all in thee, and the voice of a mill shall no more be heard at all in thee, and the light of a lamp shall shine no more at all in thee, and the voice of the bridegroom and the bride shall be heard no more at all in thee: for thy merchants were the princes of the earth; for with thy sorcery were all the nations deceived.

Popular music comes to an end in Babylon. Jazz and rock 'n roll cease in the destruction. Classical music will be stilled.

The crafts that have been prostituted to the service of the Antichrist will end. The wheels of the factories will never turn again. The bright lights of Broadway will go out forever. (It is interesting to note the beginning of all these things as recorded in Genesis 4:16-22.) Also social life and family life shall end (see Matthew 24:37,38). The great tycoons of big business will disappear.

This city deceived the world with the worship of Antichrist—this is the strong delusion.

Verse 24—And in her was found the blood of prophets, and of saints, and of all that were slain upon the earth.

This is Satan's city. He is a murderer—this city murdered. The final crime was the slaying of God's people.

As we contemplate the destruction of Babylon, we think of other great cities and civilizations of the past that have fallen.

One of the most widely read books of all time is "The Decline and Fall of the Roman Empire." Written in 1788 by Edward Gibbon it sets forth five basic reasons why that great civilization withered and died. These were:

The undermining of the dignity and sanctity of the home, which is the basis for human society.

Higher and higher taxes; the spending of public money for free bread and circuses for the populace.

The mad craze for pleasure; sports becoming every year more exciting, more brutal, more immoral.

The building of great armaments when the real enemy was within—the decay of individual responsibility.

The decay of religion; faith fading into mere form, losing touch with life, losing power to guide the people.

The oft-heard warning that "history repeats itself" has an ominous meaning in the light of the above.

The average age of the world's great civilizations has been 200 years.

These nations progressed through this sequence:

> From Bondage to Spiritual Faith
> From Spiritual Faith to Great Courage
> From Courage to Liberty
> From Liberty to Abundance
> From Abundance to Selfishness
> From Selfishness to Complacency
> From Complacency to Apathy
> From Apathy to Dependence
> From Dependence Back Again to Bondage

In 14 years the U.S. will be 200 years old. This cycle is not inevitable—
IT DEPENDS ON YOU.

Chapter 19

THEME: The marriage of the Lamb and the return of Christ in judgment.

OUTLINE:

C. Marriage of the Lamb and Return of Christ in Judgment, chapter 19

1. Four Hallelujahs, verses, 1-6
2. Bride of the Lamb and Marriage Supper, verses 7-10
3. Return of Christ as King of Kings and Lord of Lords, verses 11-16
4. Battle of Armageddon, verses 17, 18
5. Hell Opened, verses 19-21

REMARKS:

We turn the page on that which marks a drastic change in the tone of Revelation. The destruction of Babylon, the capital of the Beast's kingdom, marked the end of the Great Tribulation. The sombre gives way to song. The transfer is from darkness to light, from black to white, from dreary days of judgment to bright days of blessing.

This chapter makes a definite bifurcation in Revelation, and ushers in the greatest event for this earth—the Second Coming of Christ. It is the bridge between the Great Tribulation and the Millennium. Great and significant events are recorded here. The two central features are the marriage of the Lamb (that is, the marriage of the Lord Jesus Christ with the Church), and the return of Christ to the earth. The other events cluster about these two.

Hallelujahs open this chapter; and the opening of hell concludes it. Two great suppers are recorded—the marriage supper of the Lamb and the cannibalistic feast of carrion after the battle of Armageddon.

COMMENT:

1. Four Hallelujahs, verses, 1-6

Verse 1—And after these things I heard a great voice of much people in heaven, saying, Alleluia; Salvation, and glory, and honour, and power, unto the Lord our God.

After these things I heard as it were a great voice of a great multitude in heaven, saying, Hallelujah; Salvation, and glory, and power, unto the Lord our God.

After these things (meta tauta) brings us to the end of the Great Tribulation, and this is its last occurrence.

A great multitude includes those we have seen previously in the great worship scene in Revelation 5:8-12 and in 7:9-15. This is the first time that they have been able to utter the great note of praise of the Old Testament—*Hallelujah!* It occurs 4 times in the first 6 verses, which is the only occurrence in the New Testament. It is reserved for the final victory. It is interesting to note that *hallelujah* occurs frequently in the book of Psalms. It means "praise the Lord." It appears in frequent succession in Psalm 146 to 150. Psalm 150 is a mighty crescendo of praise. *Hallelujah* is a fitting note of praise at this juncture in Revelation.

> Let the sinners be consumed out of the earth, and let the wicked be
> no more. Bless thou the LORD, O my soul. Praise ye the LORD (Psa.
> 104:35).

Hallelujah is an expletive of praise as the final phase of salvation is coming to pass (see Romans 8:18-23).

Verses 2-4—For true and righteous are his judgments: for he hath judged the great whore, which did corrupt the earth with her fornication, and hath avenged the blood of his servants at her hand. And again they said, Alleluia. And her smoke rose up for ever and ever. And the four and twenty elders and the four beasts fell down and worshipped God that sat on the throne, saying, Amen; Alleluia.

For true and righteous are his judgments; for he hath judged the great harlot who (formerly) corrupted the earth with her fornication, and he hath avenged the blood of his servants at her hand. And the second time they said, Hallelujah. And her smoke goeth up for ever and ever. And the four and twenty elders and the four living creatures fell down and worshipped God that sitteth on the throne, saying, Amen; Hallelujah.

As long as the imposter of the true Church — the great harlot — is on the earth, the marriage of the Lamb will not take place in heaven. The anti-church is disposed of first, which makes way for the marriage of the Lamb. This points up the time of the marriage of the Lamb. The apostate church — the harlot — is destroyed in the middle of the Great Tribulation. The marriage of the Lamb takes place at that time or at some period between that and the return of Christ to the earth.

Her destruction avenges the blood of all the martyrs. The Church is forbidden to avenge herself.

> Dearly beloved, avenge not yourselves, but rather give place unto wrath: for it is written, Vengeance is mine; I will repay, saith the Lord (Rom. 12:19).

The 24 elders for the first time sing, Hallelujah. The 24 elders we believe to be the Church (see Revelation 4). This is the last time the elders appear as such, for the figure changes now, and the Church is to become the Bride of Christ. The word *church* means *called out*. Here on the earth we are the church, the called out ones, but the minute we leave the earth we are the Bride.

Verses 5, 6—And a voice came out of the throne, saying, Praise our God, all ye his servants, and ye that fear him, both small and great. And I heard as it were the voice of a great multitude, and as the voice of many waters, and as the voice of mighty thunderings, saying, Alleluia: for the Lord God omnipotent reigneth.

And a voice came forth from the throne, saying, Give praise to our God, all ye his servants, ye that fear him, the small and the great. And I heard as it were the voice of a great multitude, and as it were the voice of many waters, and as it were the voice of mighty thunders, saying, Hallelujah; for the Lord our God, the Almighty reigneth.

The call comes directly from the throne to praise God, because the Lord Jesus Christ is preparing to take control of this world. This is the true Hallelujah Chorus, and is the most profound paean of praise so far in this book. See II Samuel 7:16; Psalm 89:34-37; 45:6, 7; 72:17-20; Isaiah 9:7; Jeremiah 23:5; Matt. 25:31; Luke 1:32, 33.

2. Bride of the Lamb and MARRIAGE SUPPER, verses 7-10

Verses 7, 8—Let us be glad and rejoice, and give honour to him: for the marriage of the Lamb is come, and his wife hath made herself ready. And to her was granted that she should be arrayed in fine linen, clean and white: for the fine linen is the righteousness of saints.

Let us rejoice and be exceeding glad, and let us give the glory unto him; for the marriage of the Lamb is come, and his wife hath made herself ready. And it was given unto her that she should array herself in fine linen, bright and pure; for the fine linen is the righteous acts of the saints.

This is the most thrilling experience for the Church. She is to be presented to Christ in marriage. The marriage takes place in heaven. This is a heavenly scene. The Church, the total number of believers from the day of Pentecost down to the Rapture, is the Bride.

Husbands, love your wives, even as Christ also loved the church, and gave himself for it; that he might sanctify and cleanse it with the washing of water by the word, that he might present it to himself a glorious church, not having spot, or wrinkle, or any such thing; but that it should be holy and without blemish (Eph. 5:25-27).

Even John the Baptist designated himself as a friend of the bridegroom, yet his joy was complete.

The Bride occupies a unique position to Christ—"He loved the church and gave himself for it."

I in them, and thou in me, that they may be made perfect in one; and that the world may know that thou hast sent me, and has loved them, as thou hast loved me. Father, I will that they also, whom thou hast given me, be with me where I am; that they may behold my glory, which thou hast given me: for thou lovedst me before the foundation of the world. O righteous Father, the world hath not known thee: but I have known thee, and these have known that thou hast sent me. And I have declared unto them thy name, and will declare it: that the love wherewith thou hast loved me may be in them, and I in them (John 17:23-26).

The wedding gown of the Church is *the righteous acts of the saints.* This is a difficult concept to accept, for it is impossible for us to stand before Christ in our own righteousness. Paul wrote:

And be found in him, not having mine own righteousness, which is of the law, but that which is through the faith of Christ, the righteousness which is of God by faith (Phil. 3:9).

By faith we can trust Christ—not only for forgiveness of sins, but for the impartation to us of His righteousness. Then why does John say that the wedding garment is the righteous *acts* of the saints? The wedding gown is used but once, we will be clothed with the righteousness of Christ throughout eternity. We, as believers, will appear before the judgment seat of Christ, not to be judged for salvation, but for rewards. Through the ages, believers have been performing righteous acts which are accumulating to adorn the wedding gown. What have you been doing to adorn it?

Now if any man build upon this foundation gold, silver, precious stones, wood, hay, stubble; every man's work shall be made manifest: for the day shall declare it, because it shall be revealed by fire; and the fire shall try every man's work of what sort it is. If any man's work abide which he hath built thereupon, he shall receive a reward (I Cor. 3:12-14).

These good works are the wedding garment of the Church.

For we are his workmanship, created in Christ Jesus unto good works, which God hath before ordained that we should walk in them (Eph. 2:10).

After the wedding, the wedding dress is laid aside. We have already seen that the elders placed their crowns at the feet of the Lamb, proclaiming that He alone is worthy. The Church will reveal His glory:

That in the ages to come he might show the exceeding riches of his grace in his kindness toward us through Christ Jesus (Eph. 2:7).

The relationship of Christ and the Church is intimate, different, and delightful. No other creature will enjoy such sweetness.

Verses 9, 10—And he saith unto me, Write, Blessed are they which are called unto the marriage supper of the Lamb. And he saith unto me, These are the true sayings of God. And I fell at his feet to worship him. And he said unto me, See thou do it not: I am thy fellowservant, and of thy brethren that have the testimony of Jesus: worship God for the testimony of Jesus is the spirit of prophecy.

And he saith unto me, Write, Blessed are they that are bidden (invited) to the marriage supper of the Lamb. And he saith unto me, These are the true words of God. And I fell down before his feet to worship him. And he saith unto me, See thou do it not; I am a fellow servant with thee and with thy brethren that hold the testimony of Jesus; worship God: for the testimony of Jesus is the spirit of prophecy.

The marriage of the Lamb takes place in heaven, but the marriage supper takes place on earth. The picture in Matthew 25:1-13 of the ten virgins confirms this—after the marriage, the bridegroom returns to the earth for the marriage supper, which the ten virgins were expecting to attend. Another picture of this same scene is given in Psalm 45. In this Psalm Christ is seen coming as king. The queen is there:

Kings' daughters were among thy honourable women: upon thy right hand did stand the queen in gold of Ophir (Psa. 45:9).

Guests are present:

And the daughter of Tyre shall be there with a gift; even the rich among the people shall intreat thy favour (Psa. 45:12).

Both Israel and the Gentiles who enter the Millennium are the invited guests. The marriage supper is evidently the Millennium. At the end of the Millennium the Church is still seen as a Bride (see Revelation 21:2, 9). Imagine a honeymoon that lasts 1000 years! Yet that is only the beginning. What joy! What ecstasy! The angel puts God's seal on this scene—*These are the true words of God.*

After acting as a scribe for this scene, John feels compelled to worship the angelic messenger. However he is restrained from doing so—the angel is but a creature. Only God is to be worshipped. What a rebuke to Satan, the Antichrist, and the false prophet.

3. RETURN OF CHRIST as King of Kings and Lord of Lords, verses 11-16

Verses 11, 12—And I saw heaven opened, and behold a white horse; and he that sat upon him was called Faithful and True, and in righteousness he doth judge and make war. His eyes were as a flame of fire, and on his head were many crowns; and he had a name written, that no man knew, but he himself.

And I saw the heaven opened, and behold, a white horse, and he that sat on him was called Faithful and True, and in righteousness doth he judge and make war. Now his eyes a flame of fire, and upon his head many diadems; having a name written which none knew but himself.

This is the great climactic event toward which all things are moving. The contrast to His first coming is remarkable.

His coming is the final manifestation of the wrath of God upon a sinful world. The rebellion of Satan, demons, and men is contained, put down, and judged. He puts down all unrighteousness before He establishes His kingdom in righteousness.

Heaven is opened in Revelation 4:1 to let John enter. Here heaven opens to let Christ exit. The white horse, on which He rides, is the animal of warfare. When Jesus was on earth He rode into Jerusalem upon an ass, which, though an animal of kings, denoted peace, not war.

He is called *Faithful* because He has come to execute the long-time program of God.

He is called *True* for He is inherently true—"I am . . . the truth."

He has come to *judge and make war*—not to die on a cross. Now His eyes are a *flame*, not *as* a flame (1:14).

The many diadems indicate that He will be the sole ruler of the earth.

What is the *name* that no one knew but Himself? He is given four names here which correspond to the gospels:

(1) King of kings— Matthew
(2) Faithful and True— Mark (presented as the servant)
(3) Word of God— John
(4) .... Luke (presented as Jesus, the Son of man, "no man knoweth the Son, but the Father."

Could the name be Jesus?

Verses 13-16—And he was clothed with a vesture dipped in blood: and his name is called The Word of God. And the armies which were in heaven followed Him upon white horses, clothed in fine linen, white and clean. And out of his mouth goeth a sharp sword, that with it he should smite the nations: and he shall rule them with a rod of iron: and he treadeth the winepress of the fierceness and wrath of Almighty God. And he hath on his vesture and on his thigh a name written, KING OF KINGS, AND LORD OF LORDS.

And he is arrayed in a garment sprinkled with blood: and his name is called the Word of God. And the armies which are in heaven followed him upon white horses, clothed in fine linen, white and pure. And out of his mouth proceedeth a sharp sword, that with it he should smite the nations; and he shall rule them with a rod of iron: and he treadeth the winepress of the fierceness of the wrath of God the All-ruler. And he hath on his garment and on his thigh a name written, KING OF KINGS, AND LORD OF LORDS.

His garment is sprinkled with blood, while the garments of His armies are white and pure. He, as the Word of God, will alone execute the word of judg-ment. Isaiah has set this same scene before us in chapter 63:1-6 (see author's book, *Initiation Into Isaiah*). David also described this scene:

> Yet have I set my king upon my holy hill of Zion. I will declare the decree: the LORD hath said unto me, Thou art my Son; this day have I begotten thee. Ask of me, and I shall give thee the heathen for thine inheritance, and the uttermost parts of the earth for thy possession. Thou shalt break them with a rod of iron; thou shalt dash them in pieces like a potter's vessel (Psa. 2:6-9).

See also Psalm 45:3-7 and Isaiah 11:4.

The fury of His wrath at His second coming is in sharp contrast to His gentleness at His first coming. However, in both is revealed the "wrath of the Lamb."

The armies of heaven are evidently the legions of angels that do His bidding.

4. BATTLE OF ARMAGEDDON, verses 17, 18

Verses 17, 18—And I saw an angel standing in the sun; and he cried with a loud voice, saying to all the fowls that fly in the midst of heaven, Come and gather yourselves together unto the supper of the great God; that ye may eat the flesh of kings, and the flesh of captains, and the flesh of mighty men, and the flesh of horses, and of them that sit on them, and the flesh of all men, both free and bond, both small and great.

If there is one passage of Scripture which is revolting to read, this is it. God included it at the end of His Word to remind us how revolting and nause-ating to Him are the deeds of the flesh. Men who live in the flesh, will have their flesh destroyed. This is an invitation to the carrion-eating fowl to a ban-quet on earth where they will have blue ribbon flesh to eat.

It is frightful to rebel against God (see Matthew 24:28; Luke 17:37). This is the aftermath of the final phase of Armageddon.

5. HELL OPENED, verses 19-21

Verses 19-21—And I saw the beast, and the kings of the earth, and their armies, gathered together to make war against him that sat on the horse, and against his army. And the beast was taken, and with him the false prophet that wrought miracles before him, with which he deceived them that had received the mark of the beast, and them that worshipped his image. These both were cast alive into a lake of fire burning with brimstone. And the remnant were slain with the sword of him that sat upon the horse, which sword proceeded out of his mouth: and all the fowls were filled with their flesh.

And I saw the beast, and the kings of the earth, and their armies gathered together to make war against him that sat upon the horse and against his army. And the beast was taken, and with him the false prophet that wrought the signs in his sight, wherewith he deceived them that had received the mark of the beast and them that worshipped his image: they two were cast alive into the lake of fire that burneth with brimstone; and the rest were killed with the sword of him that sat upon the horse, even the sword which came forth out of his mouth; and all the birds were filled with their flesh.

The Beast and the False Prophet defy God right up to the very last. They dare to make war with the Son of God! Surely He that sitteth in the heavens shall laugh at the utter futility of their efforts. It is preposterous—yet such is the rebellion of man.

The outcome was inevitable. The two arch-rebels and tyrants, the Antichrist and the False Prophet, have the questionable distinction of being the first two who are cast into hell.

Is the *lake of fire* literal? If it is not, it depicts that which is worse than a fire of brimstone.

The *sword* which goes out of the mouth of the Lord Jesus, is evidently the Word of God. The Word is likened unto a sword:

> For the word of God is quick, and powerful, and sharper than any twoedged sword, piercing even to the dividing asunder of soul and spirit, and of the joints and marrow, and is a discerner of the thoughts and intents of the heart (Heb. 4:12).

> And take the helmet of salvation, and the sword of the Spirit, which is the word of God (Eph. 6:17).

> But with righteousness shall he judge the poor, and reprove with equity for the meek of the earth: and he shall smite the earth with the rod of his mouth, and with the breath of his lips shall he slay the wicked (Isa. 11:4).

Up to this point Satan has not entered hell.

Those who received the mark of the Beast are slain by the Sword of Christ. They will be raised from the dead when the other lost are raised and cast into the lake of fire (see Revelation 20:11-15).

The last section of this chapter is sombre, and should sober our thinking in this life.

Chapter 20

THEME: The Millennium in relationship to Christ, Satan, Man, Tribulation Saints; the Resurrections, the Earth, and the Great White Throne.

OUTLINE:

D. Millennium, chapter 20

1. **Satan Bound** 1000 Years, verses 1-3
2. **Saints** of the Great Tribulation **Reign** with Christ 1000 Years,
   verses 4-6
3. **Satan Loosed** After 1000 Years, verses 7-9
4. **Satan Cast** Into Lake of Fire and Brimstone, verse 10
5. **Setting of Great White Throne** Where Lost are Judged and Follow Satan into Lake of Fire and Brimstone, verses 11-15

REMARKS:

This is the most controverted chapter in the field of eschatology. Here is the division point for the three main schools of eschatology.

Postmillennialism assumed that Christ would come at the conclusion of 1000 years. Man would bring in the kingdom by the preaching of the gospel. This was an optimistic view which prevailed at the turn of the century. It has become obsolete, as it could not weather the first half of the 20th century which produced two world wars, a global depression, the rise of Communism, and the atomic bomb with which world-wide destruction is imminent.

Amillennialism has become popular only in recent years, as it largely has supplanted postmillennialism. It holds out no false optimism, and has for the most part emphasized the Coming of Christ. Its chief weakness is that it spiritualizes the 1000 years—as it does all of the book of Revelation. It fits the Millennium into the present age and all of the events recorded in Revelation into the facts of history like pieces are fitted into a crazyquilt. The results are the same.

Premillennialism, on the contrary, takes Revelation 20 at face value, as it does all of the book of Revelation, applying the literalist interpretation—unless the context instructs otherwise. The 1000 years are treated as 1000 years, and Christ comes at the beginning of the Millennium. Revelation 20 makes it clear that there can be no Millennium until Christ comes.

First of all, there can be no Millennium until Satan is removed from the earthly scene. In the second place, the curse of sin must be removed from the physical earth before a Millennium can be established (see Isaiah 11:6-9; 35:1-10; Romans 8:18-23). In the third place, the resurrection of the Old Testament saints must take place at the beginning of the 1000 years (see Daniel 12:1-2 and author's book, *Delving Through Daniel*; also Isaiah 25:8, 9). Only Christ can raise the dead (see John 5:21, 25, 28, 29). In the fourth place, the tribulation saints are included in the resurrection of the Old Testament saints (verse 4), and they reign with Christ during the Millennium. Finally, the Millennium is the final testing of man under ideal conditions. This is the answer to those who say that there is nothing wrong in man which circumstances and conditions cannot change. Man is an incurable and incorrigible sinner. Even at the end of the Millennium, he is still in rebellion against God. The rebellion in the human heart and the depraved nature of man is impossible for any man to comprehend.

The Millennium is the final testing of mankind before the beginning of the eternal state.

The Millennium is God's answer to the prayer, "Thy kingdom come." This is the kingdom promised to David (see II Samuel 7:12-17 and 23:5). God took an oath relative to its establishment (Psalm 89:34-37). This is the kingdom predicted in the Psalms (Psalm 2; 45; 110) and in the prophets (Isaiah 2:1-5; 11:1-9; 60; 61:3-62; 66; Jeremiah 23:3-8; 32:37-44; Ezekiel 40:48; Daniel 2:44. 45; 7:13, 14; 12:2, 3; Micah 4:1-8; Zechariah 12:10-14:21; also all of the Minor Prophets point to the kingdom). These are but a few of the manifold Scriptures that speak of the theocratic kingdom.

COMMENT:

1. **SATAN BOUND** 1000 Years, verses 1-3

Verses 1-3—And I saw an angel come down from heaven, having the key of the bottomless pit and a great chain in his hand. And he laid hold on the dragon, that old serpent, which is the Devil, and Satan, and bound him a thousand years, and cast him into the bottomless pit, and shut him up, and set a seal upon him, that he should deceive the nations no more, till the thousand years should be fulfilled: and after that he must be loosed a little season.

And I saw an angel coming down out of the heaven, having the key of the abyss and a great chain in his hand. And he laid hold on the dragon, the old serpent who is the Devil and Satan, and bound him for a thousand years, and cast him into the abyss, and locked and sealed (it) over, that he should deceive the nations no longer, until the thousand years should be finished: after that he must be loosed for a little time.

Many expositors separate this section from the Millennium, classifying it as the closing scene of the Day of Wrath (Newell, Govett, etc.). This view takes the edge from the sharp distinction that there will be on earth at the removal of Satan. His incarceration and total absence from the earth changes conditions from darkness to light. He is the god of this age, the prince of the power of the air, and his power and influence in the world is enormous—beyond the computing of any IBM machine. His withdrawal makes way for the Millennium —with him loose there could be no Millennium.

Satan's great power is reduced, for an ordinary angel becomes his jailor and leads him away captive (see Jude 9; Revelation 12:7-9).

The abyss is a better description of the prison than is "the bottomless pit." In either case it is not "the lake of fire" (see notes on Revelation 9:1, 2).

After that he must be loosed for a little time is one of the imponderable statements of Scripture. When the late Dr. Chafer was asked why God loosed Satan after he once had him bound, he replied, "If you will tell me why God let him loose in the first place, I will tell you why God lets him loose the second time." Apparently Satan is released at the end of the Millennium to reveal that the ideal conditions of the kingdom, under the personal reign of Christ, do not change the human heart. This reveals the enormity of the enmity of man against God. Scripture is accurate when it describes the heart as "desperately wicked" and incurably so. Man is totally depraved. The loosing of Satan at the end of the 1000 years proves it.

2. SAINTS of the Great Tribulation REIGN with Christ 1000 Years, verses 4-6

Verses 4-6—And I saw thrones, and they sat upon them, and judgment was given unto them: and I saw the souls of them that were beheaded for the witness of Jesus, and for the word of God, and which had not worshipped the beast, neither his image, neither had received his mark upon their foreheads, or in their hands; and they lived and reigned with Christ a thousand years. But the rest of the dead lived not again until the thousand years were finished. This is the first resurrection. Blessed and holy is he that hath part in the first resurrection: on such the second death hath no power, but they shall be priests of God and of Christ, and shall reign with him a thousand years.

And I saw thrones and they sat upon them, and judgment was given unto them; and (I saw) the souls of them that had been beheaded for the testimony of Jesus, and for the Word of God; and whosoever worshipped not the wild beast neither his image, and received not the mark upon their forehead, or upon their hand. And they lived again and reigned with Christ one thousand years. This is the first resurrection. Blessed and holy is he that hath part in the first resurrection; over these the second death hath no authority (exousian), but they shall be priests of God and of the Christ, and shall reign with him a thousand years.

When this passage is treated as a dignified statement of literal facts, it becomes reasonable and fits into the form of prophecy:

> Knowing this first, that no prophecy of the scripture is of any private interpretation (II Peter 1:20).

Any attempt to reduce it to the lowest common denominator of fanciful and figurative symbols makes the passage an absurdity. To spiritualize this passage is to disembowel all Scripture of vital meaning. making the interpretation of Scripture a *reductio ad absurdum*.

The thrones are literal; the martyrs are literal; Jesus is literal; and the Word of God is literal; the Beast is literal; the image is literal; the mark of the Beast is literal; their foreheads and their hands are literal; the 1000 years are literal; the resurrection is literal. The word for resurrection is *anastasei* which means to stand up. It is rather difficult for a spirit to stand up, and those who spiritualize this section are at a loss to explain just how a spirit stands up. This is the same word used in I Corinthians 15 for the resurrection of Christ and believers.

And I saw thrones and they sat upon them is the one statement that is not entirely clear. Who are "they?" They must be the total number of those who have part in the first resurrection. which includes all the saved of all ages.

The first resurrection began with the resurrection of Christ; then followed the resurrection of His Church 1900 (plus) years afterward—but before the Great Tribulation (Revelation 4). At the end of the Great Tribulation is the resurrection of both the tribulation saints ("the souls of them that had been beheaded for the testimony of Jesus, and for the Word of God; and whoever worshipped not the beast . . . etc."), and the Old Testament saints (Daniel

12:1, 2). The diagram that follows gives the resurrection as a parade. Christ, the first fruit of resurrection, leads the parade:

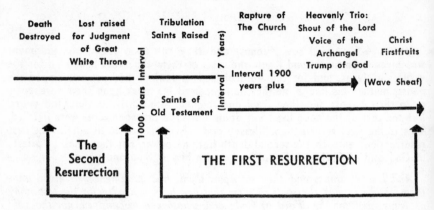

The tribulation saints and the Old Testament saints will evidently reign on this earth with Christ. David will be His vice gerent.

The Church, which is the Bride of Christ, will reside in the New Jerusalem, where she reigns with Him from that exalted place. Christ will commute back and forth from the New Jerusalem to the earth. In fact, there must be a great deal of traffic as the Church travels back and forth between its heavenly home and the earth. Multitudes of both Israel and the Gentiles will enter the kingdom in natural bodies, not having died. These are the ones who are tested during this period. As Christ in a glorified body mingled with His apostles and followers, so the Church will mingle with these multitudes in their natural bodies.

They shall be priests unto God refers to the entire nation of Israel. This was God's original purpose with Israel:

And ye shall be unto me a kingdom of priests, and an holy nation. These are the words which thou shalt speak unto the children of Israel (Exodus 19:6).

Abraham was a priest in his family; Levi was the priestly tribe, with the family of Aaron serving as high priest; and in the theocratic kingdom the entire nation of Israel will be priests.

In Scripture there is more prophecy concerning the Millennium than of any other period. The kingdom was the theme of the Old Testament prophets.

3. SATAN LOOSED After 1000 Years, verses 7-9

Verses 7-9—And when the thousand years are expired, Satan shall be loosed out of his prison, and shall go out to deceive the nations which are in the four quarters of the earth, Gog and Magog to gather them together to battle: the number of whom is as the sand of the sea. And they went up on the breadth of the earth, and compassed the camp of the saints about, and the beloved city: and fire came down from God out of heaven, and devoured them.

And when the thousand years are ended Satan shall be loosed out of his prison, and shall come forth to deceive the nations which are in the four corners (quarters) of the earth, Gog and Magog, to gather them together to the war; the number of whom is as the sand of the sea. And they went up over the breadth of the earth, and compassed the camp of the saints about, and the beloved city: and fire came down out of heaven, and devoured them.

Although the entire book of Revelation deals with last things, especially do these last few chapters. Here is the last rebellion of Satan and man against God. The Millennium is a time of testing of man under ideal conditions—as this passage demonstrates. As soon as Satan is released, a great company, who have been under the personal reign of Christ under ideal circumstances, goes over to him. From where did such a company come? is a worthy question. The answer lies in the fact that not only do multitudes *enter* the Millennium, but multitudes are *born* during the Millennium (see Isaiah 11:6; 65:20). This will be the time of earth's greatest population explosion. Disease will be eliminated; and since the curse of sin will be removed from the physical earth, it will produce enough foodstuff to feed its greatest population. The human heart alone remains unchanged, and many will chafe under the righteous rule of Christ. He will be an absolute monarch, unparalleled by any dictator. This explains why the mob will go over to Satan. The nations of the earth will again come under the spell of Satan, and will plot a rebellion.

Because the rebellion is labeled "Gog and Magog," many Bible students identify it with Gog and Magog of Ezekiel 38 and 39. This, of course, is not possible, for the conflicts described are not parallel as to time, place, or participants—only the name is the same.

The invasion from the north by Gog and Magog of Ezekiel 38 and 39, breaks the false peace of the Antichrist and causes him to show his hand in the midst of the Great Tribulation. That rebellion of the godless forces from the north will have made such an impression on mankind, that after 1000 years the last rebellion of man bears the same label. We have passed through a similar situation in this century. World War I was so devastating that when war again broke out in Europe, it was labeled again World War, but differentiated by the number 2. Now World War III is being predicted. Likewise the war in Ezekiel 38 and 39 is Gog and Magog I, while this reference in verse 8 is to Gog and Magog II.

In verse 9 there is the dropping of the last atomic bomb. The phrase "from God" is not in the best texts. It simply means that natural forces which destroyed Gog and Magog I will destroy Gog and Magog II. This last rebellion and resistance against God was as foolish and futile as man's first rebellion in the Garden of Eden. Here it is not the beginning but the ending of man's disobedience to God. It is the finality of man's rebellion—nothing remains but the final judgment.

4. SATAN CAST Into the Lake of Fire and Brimstone, verse 10

Verse 10—And the devil that deceived them was cast into the lake of fire and brimstone, where the beast and the false prophet are, and shall be tormented day and night for ever and ever.

And the devil that deceived them was cast into the lake of fire and brimstone, where are also the wild beast and the false prophet; and they shall be tormented day and night for ever and ever.

This is a most solemn statement; yet it is a relief to God's child to know that the enemy—both his and God's—will at last be brought to permanent justice. There is nothing here to satisfy the curiosity or the sadistic taste. The fact is stated in reverent reticence which is awe-inspiring.

Several facts here contradict popular notions. First, the devil is not in hell today. In the second place, he is not the first to be cast into hell. The Wild Beast and the False Prophet precede him by 1000 years. Finally, hell is described as a lake of fire and brimstone. The Lord Jesus is the one who gave the most solemn description of hell:

> Then said he to the multitude that came forth to be baptized of him, O generation of vipers, who hath warned you to flee from the wrath to come (Luke 3:7)?
>
> For I have five brethren; that he may testify unto them, lest they also come into this place of torment(Luke 16:28).
>
> Then shall he say also unto them on the left hand, Depart from me, ye cursed, into everlasting fire, prepared for the devil and his angels (Matthew 25:41).
>
> But the children of the kingdom shall be cast out into outer darkness: there shall be weeping and gnashing of teeth (Matt. 8:12).
>
> And shall cast them into a furnace of fire; there shall be wailing and gnashing of teeth (Matt. 13:42).
>
> Where their worm dieth not, and the fire is not quenched (Mark 9:44).

These descriptions cannot be reduced to something less, nor can they be dissolved into the thin air of make-believe. The reality far exceeds the description; and human language is beggarly in trying to depict the awful reality. Hell is a place; it is also a state. It is a place of conscious torment.

5. SETTING OF GREAT WHITE THRONE Where Lost are Judged and Follow Satan into Lake of Fire and Brimstone, verses 11-15

Verse 11—And I saw a great white throne, and him that sat on it, from whose face the earth and the heaven fled away; and there was found no place for them.

And I saw a great white throne, and Him that sat upon it, from whose face the earth and the heaven fled away; and there was found no place for them.

The Great White Throne is what men mistakenly call the general judgment. It is general only in the sense that all the *lost* of all ages are raised to be judged here. All the *saved* have been raised in the first resurrection, and have been judged and properly rewarded. Here the lost are raised to be given an equitable, fair and just evaluation of their works in respect to their salvation.

The holiness of this throne is revealed in the reaction of heaven and earth to it—they roll up as a scroll. The One sitting on the throne is the Lord Jesus Christ.

> For the Father judgeth no man, but hath committed all judgment unto the Son. . . . For as the Father hath life in himself; so hath he given to the Son to have life in himself; and hath given him authority to execute judgment also, because he is the Son of man. Marvel not at this: for the hour is coming, in the which all that are in the graves

shall hear his voice, and shall come forth; they that have done good, unto the resurrection of life; and they that have done evil, unto the resurrection of damnation (John 5:22, 26-29).

Verses 12, 13—And I saw the dead, small and great, stand before God; and the books were opened: and another book was opened, whirh is the book of life: and the dead were judged out of those things which were written in the books, according to their works. And the sea gave up the dead which were in it; and death and hell delivered up the dead which were in them: and they were judged every man according to their works.

And I saw the dead, great and the small, standing before the throne; and books were opened; and another book was opened, which is the book of life; and the dead were judged out of the things which were written in the books, according to their works. And the sea gave up the dead that were in it; and death and Hades gave up the dead that were in them; and they were judged every one according to their works.

And I saw is the fourfold repetition of John in this chapter to remind us that he is a spectator to these events.

The dead are classified as the small and the great. They are all lost, for evidently none have their names written in the book of life. They had never turned to God for salvation. The Lord Jesus said that in his generation, "ye will not come to me that ye may have life." These had not come.

There are books which record the works of all individuals. If man can make electronic computers which give an accurate account of men's affairs, surely God will have no problem in doing so.

Multitudes want to be judged according to their works. This is their opportunity. The judgment is just, but no one is saved by works.

The sea gave up the dead that were in it. Multitudes, who have gone to a watery grave in which the chemicals of their bodies have been dissolved in the waters of the sea, will be raised. The graves on earth will give up their bodies, and Hades, the place where the spirits of the lost go, will disgorge for this judgment.

Verses 14, 15—And death and hell were cast into the lake of fire. This is the second death. And whosoever was not found written in the book of life was cast into the lake of fire.

And death and Hades were cast into the lake of fire. This is the second death even the lake of fire. And if any were not found written in the book of life, he was cast into the lake of fire.

Death — the body will be raised from the grave.
Hell — the spirit will come back from hades and will be reunited with the body. Man will so stand before God's throne and receive his judgment.

Sheol or Hades (translated Hell in the New Testament) is divided into two compartments: Paradise and the place of torment (Luke 16:19-31). Paradise was emptied when Christ took with Him at His ascension the Old Testament believers (Eph. 4:8-10). The place of torment will deliver up the lost for judgment at the Great White Throne. All who stand at this judgment are lost, and they will be cast into the lake of fire, which is the second death.

Sheol or Hades (translated Hell in the New Testament)

to Heaven
with Christ

Paradise

Place of Torment

to
Lake of Fire

(the first to go here are the Beast and the False Prophet, Rev. 19:20; then Satan, 20:10; and finally all who were not found written in the book of life, 20:15).

Death, the great final enemy of man, is finally removed from the scene. No longer will it be said, "In Adam all die." Death is personified in this case, for it is man's great enemy.

I will ransom them from the power of the grave; I will redeem them from death: O death, I will be thy plagues; O grave, I will be thy destruction: repentance shall be hid from mine eyes (Hosea 13:14).

The last enemy that shall be destroyed is death. . . . O death, where is thy sting? O grave, where is thy victory (I Cor. 15:25, 55)?

Hades, the prison of lost souls, is likewise cast into the lake of fire. The lost are no longer in Hades, but are in the lake of fire. This is where Satan, the Wild Beast, the False Prophet and their minions were consigned. If man will not accept the life of God, he must accept the only other alternative—eternal association with Satan. The second death means eternal and absolute separation from God.

Chapter 21

THEME: Eternity is unveiled—a new heaven, a new earth, a New Jerusalem, a new era, and the eternal abode of the Lamb's Bride.

OUTLINE:

E. Entrance Into Eternity; Eternity Unveiled, chapters 21, 22

1. New Heaven, New Earth, New Jerusalem, verses 1, 2
2. New Era, verses 3-8
3. New Jerusalem, Description of the Eternal Abode of the Bride, verses 9-21
4. New Relationship—God Dwelling with Man, verses 22, 23
5. New Center of the New Creation, verses 24-27

REMARKS:

Adopting a popular aphorism of the day, it can truly be said that this chapter is "out of this world." As the long vista of eternity is before us in this chapter, we have moved not only from time to eternity but into a new creation. A new heaven, a new earth, and a new Jerusalem greet us. The redeemed have previously received glorified bodies like Christ's (see I John 3:2). All things have become new.

A new universe suggests new methods and approaches to life. New laws will regulate the new universe. Here are some of the changes, suggested by Revelation 21 and 22:

(1) There will be the total absence of sin and temptation in the new creation. This in itself makes a radical difference.

(2) The New Jerusalem coming down from God out of heaven does not mean another satellite for the earth, but rather the earth and the new creation will revolve about the New Jerusalem.

(3) The law of gravity, as we know it, will be radically revised. There will be traffic between the New Jerusalem and the earth.

(4) There will be no sun to give light, for God himself will supply it directly to the universe. There will be the absence, therefore, of night.

(5) There will be no longer any sea on the earth. The sea occupies most of the earth's surface today—approximately ¾ of the total surface is water. This denotes a revolution in life upon the earth. There will be no fish to eat. Apparently man will be a vegetarian in the Millennium, as he was in the Garden of Eden. Fruits is on the diet of the eternal man (Revelation 22:2).

(6) The presence of Christ and God, together with the throne of God made visible, ushers in a new day for man—the new creation.

COMMENT:

1. New Heaven, New Earth, New Jerusalem, verses 1, 2

Verse 1—And I saw a new heaven and a new earth: for the first heaven and the first earth were passed away; and there was no more sea.

And I saw a new heaven and a new earth: for the first heaven and the first earth passed away: and the sea is no more.

And I saw is the oft repeated statement of John to remind us that he was a spectator to all of these scenes. He is a witness to this panoramic final scene which ushers in eternity.

The Scripture clearly teaches that this present order of creation is to pass away in order to make room for a new heaven and a new earth. The Lord Jesus Christ Himself said. "Heaven and earth shall pass away. . . ." The old creation was made for the first Adam. The Last Adam has a new creation for His new creatures.

> For, behold, I create new heavens and a new earth: and the former shall not be remembered, nor come into mind (Isaiah 65:17).

> For as the new heavens and the new earth, which I will make, shall remain before me, saith the LORD, so shall your seed and your name remain (Isaiah 66:22).

God had promised Abraham a land forever and David a throne forever; and Daniel propheised of a "kingdom which shall never be destroyed." The new earth will see the total fulfillment of these prophecies.

> These all died in faith, not having received the promises, but having seen them afar off, and were persuaded of them, and embraced them, and confessed that they were strangers and pilgrims on the earth. For they that say such things declare plainly that they seek a country. And truly, if they had been mindful of that country from whence they came out, they might have had opportunity to have returned. But now they desire a better country. that is, an heavenly: wherefore God is not ashamed to be called their God: for he hath prepared for them a city (Heb. 11:13-16).

> Nevertheless we, according to his promise, look for new heavens and a new earth. wherein dwelleth righteousness (II Peter 3:13).

Peter declares plainly, in the third chapter of his second epistle, that the present earth on which we live will be destroyed by fire:

> But the heavens and the earth, which are now, by the same word are kept in store, reserved unto fire against the day of judgment and perdition of ungodly men. . . . But the day of the Lord will come as a thief in the night: in the which the heavens shall pass away with a great noise, and the elements shall melt with fervent heat. the earth also and the works that are therein shall be burned up. Seeing then that all these things shall be dissolved, what manner of persons ought ye to be in all holy conversation and godliness (II Peter 3:7, 10, 11).

(See the author's book, *Three Worlds in One*.)

The chief characteristic of the new earth is the absence of the sea. This would automatically change the climate. atmosphere, and living conditions. It is impossible for the human mind to comprehend the great transformations which will take place in a new creation.

The sea in the past has been a barrier and a border for mankind—which in some cases has been good and in others bad. Also the sea was an instrument of judgment at the time of the flood. However, by the disappearance of the sea the population of the earth can be doubled again and again because of the increase of the land surface.

Verse 2—And I John saw the holy city, new Jerusalem, coming down from God out of heaven, prepared as a bride adorned for her husband.

And I saw the holy city, new Jerusalem, coming down out of heaven from God, made ready as a bride adorned for her husband.

And I saw reveals that John is both auditor and spectator.

The New Jerusalem is not to be identified with the earthly Jerusalem. If it existed before the eternal creation begins, there is no identification of it. John sees it descending to a position in the new heavens, and in relationship to the earth. This is evidently the place which Christ prepared for His own Church:

> In my Father's house are many mansions: if it were not so, I would have told you. I go to prepare a place for you (John 14:2).

With Christ and God dwelling there, it will become the new center of the new creation. If there is any revolving, it will be about the New Jerusalem.

Since the city is the eternal dwelling place of the Bride, both are considered synonymously. The city is as a bride adorned for her husband. The wedding garment is no longer in evidence, but after 1000 years the honeymoon is not over.

2. New Era, verses 3-8

Verses 3, 4—And I heard a great voice out of heaven saying, Behold, the tabernacle of God is with men, and he will dwell with them, and they shall be his people, and God himself shall be with them, and be their God. And God shall wipe away all tears from their eyes; and there shall be no more death, neither sorrow, nor crying, neither shall there be any more pain: for the former things are passed away.

And I heard a great voice out of the throne saying, Behold the tabernacle (skene) of God (is) with men, and He shall tabernacle with them, and they shall be His peoples, and God himself shall be with them, and be their God; and God shall wipe away every tear from their eyes; and death shall be no more, neither shall there be mourning, nor crying nor pain, any more; the first things are passed away.

And I heard is the oft repeated reminder.

A great voice out of the throne reveals that this is an authoritative communication directly from the throne of God.

Behold the tabernacle (skene) of God (is) with men, and He shall tabernacle (skenosei) with them should be compared with John 1:14, "And the Word (logos) was made (was born) flesh, and tabernacled (eskenosen) among us." The flesh of the Lord Jesus was a tabernacle whereby God came among men. In the New Jerusalem the glorified body of Jesus will be the tabernacle. He will be in a body dwelling with His Church throughout eternity. He is the only member of the trinity who dwells in a body, and He is the only man who is God. He is the God-man, the unique Being of eternity, and the object of all worship.

Peoples indicates that there will be more (see verse 26) than the Bride, the Church, who will worship and adore Him. Israel and the nations join in worship (see verse 24 and 7:9-17).

Tears, death, mourning, crying and pain will be removed from the new creation. All these belong to the first creation because of Adam's sin.

Verses 5-7—And he that sat upon the throne said, Behold, I make all things new. And he said unto me, Write: for these words are true and faithful. And he said unto me, It is done. I am Alpha and Omega, the beginning and the end. I will give unto him that is athirst of the fountain of the water of life freely. He that overcometh shall inherit all things; and I will be his God, and he shall be my son.

And he that sitteth on the throne said, Behold, I make all things new. And he saith, Write, for these words are faithful and true. And he said unto me, They are come to pass. I am the Alpha and the Omega, the beginning and the end. I will give unto him that is athirst of the fountain of the water of life freely. He that overcometh shall inherit these things; and I will be God unto him, and he shall be the son to me.

Behold I make all things new is the first declaration of God, and is comparable to Genesis 1:1. John is commanded to write because these words are not only faithful and true, but they are the same as fulfilled—"they are come to pass." God speaks of what He is going to do as if it is already done. In this same sense, Christ was the Lamb slain before the foundation of the world.

I am the Alpha and the Omega, the beginning and the end identifies the speaker as the Lord Jesus Christ (see Revelation 1:5-8).

Believers in their new bodies will thirst after God and the things of God—and they will be satisfied:
Blessed are they which do hunger and thirst after righteousness: for they shall be filled (Mat. 5:6).

All believers are overcomers because of faith:
For whatsoever is born of God overcometh the world: and this is the victory that overcometh the world, even our faith (I John 5:4).

All the Sons of God became sons through faith in Christ:
But as many as received him, to them gave he power to become the sons of God, even to them that believe on his name (John 1:12).

They *inherit all things* because this was promised to the sons of God:
The Spirit itself beareth witness with our spirit, that we are the children of God: and if children, then heirs; heirs of God, and joint-heirs with Christ; if so be that we suffer with him, that we may be also glorified together (Rom. 8:16,17).

The son to me is in the Greek *moi ho huios*. Vincent calls attention to the fact that this is the only place in John's writings where a believer is said to be a son (*huios*) in relationship with God. Believers in the Church are one of the peoples of God, but they are more—they are the sons of God in a unique and glorious fashion (see I John 3:2).

Verse 8—But the fearful, and unbelieving, and the abominable, and murderers, and whoremongers, and sorcerers, and idolaters, and all liars, shall have their part in the lake which burneth with fire and brimstone: which is the second death.

But for the fearful, and unbelieving, and defiled with abominations, and murderers, and fornicators, and sorcerers, and idolaters, and all liars, their part (shall be) in the lake that burneth with fire and brimstone: which is the second death.

There are several amazing features about this passage. First of all, the creation of new heavens and a new earth did not affect or change the status of the lake of fire and of the lost. In the second place, there is no possibility of the sin which made men become fearful, unbelieving, liars, murderers, etc., ever breaking over the barrier into the new heavens and the new earth. Sin and its potential are forever shut out of the new creation. Finally, the lake of fire is eternal, for it is the second death—and there is no third resurrection. It is eternal separation from God.

3. New Jerusalem, Description of the Eternal Abode of the Bride,
verses 9-21

Verses 9-11—And there came unto me one of the seven angels which had the seven vials full of the seven last plagues, and talked with me, saying, Come hither, I will show thee the bride, the Lamb's wife. And he carried me away in the spirit to a great and high mountain, and shewed me that great city, the holy Jerusalem, descending out of heaven from God, having the glory of God: and her light was like unto a stone most precious, even like a jasper stone, clear as crystal.

And there came one of the seven angels who had the seven bowls, who were laden with the seven last plagues; and he spoke with me, saying, Come hither, I will show thee the bride, the wife of the Lamb. And he carried me away in the Spirit to a mountain great and high, and showed me the holy city Jerusalem, coming down out of heaven from God, having the glory of God: her light was like unto a stone most precious, as it were a jasper stone, shining like crystal.

One of the seven angels who had the seven bowls is identical with Revelation 17:1, which does not imply that this scene is millennial. It merely reveals the continuity of the book of Revelation. Though we have shifted from time to eternity, there is a bridge between the two which is both logical and chronological. This angel, who had previously conducted John on a guided tour of Babylon in time, now guides him on a tour of the holy Jerusalem in eternity. This, likewise, reveals that God's program leads from darkness to dawn, from wrath to blessing. Judgment is not an end in itself. Weeping is for the night but joy cometh in the morning.

The Lord Jesus Christ is still identified as the *Lamb.* That is His eternal name and office. He is the Lamb slain before the foundation of the world (see Rev. 13:8).

The *Bride* is the Church. The Bride and the holy city Jerusalem are made synonymous, because this city is the eternal home of the Church. As Saul was identified as Saul of Tarsus—since Tarsus was his home town, so the Church and the new Jerusalem are identical for the same reason.

The New *Jerusalem* was in existence before the beginning of eternity, as it is the place Christ is preparing for His Church; but it does not come into John's view until eternity begins. The city takes its place as the center of the new creation and the source of light and life for the new universe. In the days of John, men thought that the universe was geocentric (earth centered). Humanism today makes the universe anthropocentric (man centered). The Scripture teaches that today the universe is uranocentric (heaven centered). In eternity the new universe will be Christocentric (Christ centered) and theocentric (God centered).

This city is also the wedding ring of the Church, for it is similar to our diamond—as the next expression indicates.

Jasper stone is evidently the diamond (see Revelation 4:3). *Shining like crystal* rather than "clear as crystal" further confirms it.

Verses 12-16—And had a wall great and high, and had twelve gates, and at the gates twelve angels, and names written thereon, which are the names of the twelve tribes of the children of Israel: on the east three gates; on the north three gates; on the south three gates; and on the west three gates. And the wall of the city had twelve foundations, and in them the names of the twelve apostles of the Lamb. And he that talked with me had a golden reed to measure the city, and the gates thereof, and the wall thereof. And the city lieth foursquare, and the length is as large as the breadth: and he measured the city with the reed, twelve thousand furlongs. The length and the breadth and the height of it are equal.

Having a wall great and high; having twelve (large) gates, and at the gates twelve angels; and names written thereon, which are the names of the twelve tribes of the children of Israel: on the east (day spring) were three gates; and on the north three gates; and on the south three gates; and on the west three gates. And the wall of the city had twelve foundations, and on them twelve names of the twelve apostles of the Lamb. And he that spoke with me had for a measure a golden reed to measure the city, and the gates thereof, and the wall thereof. And the city lieth foursquare, and the length thereof is as great as the breadth: and he measured the city with the reed, twelve thousand furlongs: the length and the breadth and the height thereof are equal.

The shape of this city is difficult to describe, due largely to our inability to translate our concepts from a universe of time to the new creation of eternity. For a full description of this city see the appendix after chapter 22, entitled, *The Shape of Things to Come.* This is the author's own private opinion as to the appearance of the New Jerusalem. All sorts of interpretations of this passage have been suggested. Some have envisioned it as a cube; others as a pyramid.

In view of the fact that it is hanging in space as a planet or star, it seems that it would be a globe. This is based on the assumption that there is space in the new creation. We know that time dissolves into eternity, and it is logical to conclude that space likewise dissolves into something of a higher value. Any explanation must be in the nature of speculation. The three dimensional character of the city poses the problem, which we believe can be solved only by conceiving of the city as a sphere in the shape of the earth and planets. It will be the sun for the universe, as the glory of God shines directly through its transparent foundations.

The city is inside the globe which would necessitate a globe almost the size of the earth. Roughly the city is a 1500 mile cube. This means that the inhabitants live on the inside of the globe rather than on the outside. The foundations would be the outer surface. The shape would be something like the diagram to be found in the appendix of this book.

The light would shine through the 12 foundations, giving a fantastic and startling coloring to the new universe.

Vincent gives the exact measurements of the twelve thousand furlongs as 1378.97 miles—roughly 1500 miles.

The names of the twelve tribes of Israel on the gates indicate that Israel has access to this city, as do the Gentiles (verse 26). The arrangement is identical to the tribes encamped about the tabernacle when Israel was on the wilderness march under Moses. This city is the Holy of Holies (it is foursquare like the holy of holies in the tabernacle) for the nation Israel, which here enters into the very presence of God—but as the high priest of old, does not dwell there. They come bringing their worship and glory, and then return to the earth.

It is appropriate that the names of the twelve apostles appear on the 12 foundations, for the Church is built on the foundation which the apostles laid (see Eph. 2:20 in the author's book on Ephesians).

Verses 17-21—And he measured the wall thereof, an hundred and forty and four cubits, according to the measure of a man, that is, of the angel. And the building of the wall of it was of jasper: and the city was pure gold, like unto clear glass. And the foundations of the wall of the city were garnished with all manner of precious stones. The first foundation was jasper; the second, sapphire; the third, a chalcedony; the fourth, an emerald; the fifth, sardonyx; the sixth, sardius; the seventh, chrysolite, the eighth, beryl; the ninth, a topaz; the tenth, a chrysoprasus; the eleventh, a jacinth; the twelfth, an amethyst. And the twelve gates were twelve pearls; every several gate was of one pearl: and the street of the city was pure gold, as it were transparent glass.

This further description of the city reveals how absolutely dazzling and fabulous is this city. The multi-colored display is exciting and breathtaking.

The literal character of the city is evident by the definition and description. *And he measured the wall thereof, a hundred and forty and four cubits.* Vincent defines a cubit in these terms:

> The word originally means that part of the arm between the hand and the elbowjoint, the *forearm.* Hence a *cubit* or *ell,* a measure of distance from the joint of the elbow to the tip of the middle finger, i.e., about a foot and a half. The precise length, however, is disputed. Cubit is from the Latin *cubitus the elbow,* on which one *reclines* (*cubat*).

Reckoning a cubit as a foot and a half, the wall is about 216 feet thick. That is the surface of the globe, in which the Church resides.

From the outside, the city looks like a diamond. The gold is transparent and the diamond is the setting for the gold on the inside. The fact that the street is paved with pure gold is not the chief characteristic of the city. It only reveals that gold in the New Jerusalem is comparable to asphalt and cement today. There will be a higher standard than gold in eternity.

The foundations, beginning with the outside, are as follows:

(1) jasper—perhaps the blue diamond,
(2) sapphire—opaque with a greenish or yellowish color,
(3) chalcedony—perhaps green,

(4) emerald—green,
(5) sardonyx—white and yellow (fingernail),
(6) sardius—red,
(7) chrysolite—golden lustre,
(8) beryl—sea green, aqua,
(9) topaz—greenish yellow,
(10) chrysoprasus—golden green,
(11) jacinth—violet,
(12) amethyst—purple or rose red.

> The king's daughter is all glorious within: her clothing is of wrought gold (Psalm 45:13).

Note the chapter in the appendix on *The Shape of Things to Come*.

The New Jerusalem will not be a bland, sterile, dull, and colorless place. It will be thrilling and there will not be a time when those who behold it will not gasp in awe and wonder.

The names of the twelve tribes may be inscribed on the twelve gates, but the important feature is the material of construction. Each is a perfect pearl. This is the one jewel that sets forth the Church.

> Again, the kingdom of heaven is like unto a merchant man, seeking goodly pearls: who, when he had found one pearl of great price, went and sold all that he had, and bought it (Matt. 13:45, 46).

The Church is the pearl of great price. The comparison of the Church to the formation of a pearl is striking and suggestive. The pearl is different from all other precious gems, for instead of coming from the earth, the pearl comes from the sea. Other stones are mined from the earth, found in rock and ore. They are taken out, cut, and polished to reveal their beauty. But the pearl comes out of the sea, and it comes from a living organism. A little grain of sand or some other particle begins to cut into the side of a living organism. To protect itself, the organism sends out a fluid to coat the object. Layer upon layer coats it until a beautiful pearl is formed.

The New Jerusalem is the home of the Church, and the gates of pearl are there to remind us throughout eternity that we were a little grain of sharp, dirty sand that was a hurt in the side of Christ. We were not attractive: we were in rebellion against God, walking according to the course of this world. But Christ took that ugly thing—which was you—and covered it with His righteousness. You and I are covered with Him. The beauty is not in the grain of sand, but in what the organism puts around it. God sees us in Christ, and He is lovely.

The pearl was lightly esteemed by Israel, but was precious to the Gentiles. We have no value in ourselves, yet we are the pearl of great price. The price that is put upon a thing gives it its value. The merchant man, who is Christ, sold all that He had to buy the pearl. The price that He paid gives us value. Christ gave His life to get us, and to Him we are precious.

4. New Relationship—God Dwelling with Man, verses 22, 23

Verses 22, 23—And I saw no temple therein: for the Lord God Almighty and the Lamb are the temple of it. And the city had no need of the sun, neither of the moon, to shine in it: for the glory of God did lighten it, and the Lamb is the light thereof.

And I saw no temple therein: for the Lord God the Almighty, and the Lamb, are the temple thereof. And the city hath no need of the sun, neither of the moon to shine upon it: for the glory of God did lighten it, and the lamp thereof is the Lamb.

God lights the new creation directly by His presence. After the entrance of sin into the old creation, God withdrew His presence and "darkness covered the face of the deep." Then God made use of the physical lights in His universe. However, in the new creation, sin is removed and He becomes again the source of light. Today the Lord Jesus Christ is the light of the world in a spiritual sense.

> Then spake Jesus again unto them, saying, I am the light of the world: he that followeth me shall not walk in darkness, but shall have the light of life (John 8:12).

In the new creation, He is the direct physical as well as spiritual light. In the tabernacle there was the golden lampstand, which is one of the finest pictures of Christ. In the New Jerusalem, He *is* the golden lampstand. The nations of the world will enter the holy city as the priests entered the holy place in the tabernacle for the purpose of worship. The nations of the earth, as well as Israel, will come to the New Jerusalem as the high priest of old entered the holy of holies. Instead of the blood being brought, the Lamb is there in person.

5. New Center of the New Creation, verses 24-27

Verses 24-27—And the nations of them which are saved shall walk in the light of it: and the kings of the earth do bring their glory and honour into it. And the gates of it shall not be shut at all by day: for there shall be no night there. And they shall bring the glory and honour of the nations into it. And there shall in no wise enter into it anything that defileth, neither whatsoever worketh abomination, or maketh a lie: but they which are written in the Lamb's book of life.

And the nations shall walk amidst the light thereof: and the kings of the earth bring their glory into it. And the gates thereof shall in no wise be shut by day (for there shall be no night there): and they shall bring the glory and the honor of the nations into it: and there shall in no wise enter into it anything unclean, or he that maketh an abomination and a lie: but only they that are written in the Lamb's book of life.

God has apparently accomplished His original purpose with man—fellowship. He now has a creature who is a free moral agent and who chooses to worship and serve Him eternally.

There can be no night, since the Lamb is the light, and He is eternally present.

The gates are not for protection, as they are never closed. Rather, they are the badge or coat of arms of the Church. The pearl of great price has been purchased at great price. The Church will be for the display of His grace.

> That in the ages to come he might show the exceeding riches of his grace in his kindness toward us through Christ Jesus (Eph. 2:7).

The Church will be the fairest jewel of all when He makes up His jewels (Mal. 3:17, 18).

The Lamb's book of life contains the names of the redeemed of all ages. No one who was not redeemed by the blood of Christ will be permitted ever to enter the portals of the New Jerusalem. There is a great gulf fixed between saved and lost.

The greatest joy that will capture the heart of the redeemed will be that of abiding in the presence of Christ for eternity—"that where I am there ye may be also." This is heaven.

Chapter 22

THEME: The river of the water of life, the tree of life, the promise of Christ's return repeated, and the final invitation of the Bible.

OUTLINE:

E. Entrance Into Eternity; Eternity Unveiled, chapters 21, 22 (continued)

6. River of the Water of Life and the Tree of Life, verses 1-5
7. Promise of the Return of Christ, verses 6-16
8. Final Invitation and Warning, verses 17-19
9. Final Promise and Prayer, verses 20, 21

REMARKS:

This chapter brings us to the final scenes of this great book of scenic wonders. It likewise brings us to the end of the Word of God. God gives us His final words here and because they are last words, they have a greater significance. We are brought to the end of man's journey. The path has been rugged, and many questions remain unanswered and many problems remain unsolved; but man enters eternity in fellowship again with God. All will be answered.

The Bible opens with God on the scene, "In the beginning God created the heaven and the earth"; it concludes with Him on the scene and in full control of His own. He suffered, He paid a price, and He died—but the victory and the glory are His. He is satisfied.

> He shall see of the travail of his soul, and shall be satisfied: by his knowledge shall my righteous servant justify many; for he shall bear their iniquities (Isa. 53:11).

COMMENT:

6. River of the Water of Life and the Tree of Life, verses 1-5

Verses 1, 2—And he shewed me a pure river of water of life, clear as crystal, proceeding out of the throne of God and of the Lamb. In the midst of the street of it, and on either side of the river, was there the tree of life, which bare twelve manner of fruits, and yielded her fruit every month: and the leaves of the tree were for the healing of the nations.

And he showed me a river of water of life, bright as crystal, proceeding out of the throne of God and of the Lamb. In the midst of the street thereof. And on this side of the river and on that was the tree of life, bearing twelve fruits, yielding its fruit every month: and the leaves of the tree were for the healing of the nations.

Up to this chapter, the New Jerusalem seems to be all mineral and no vegetable. Its appearance is as the dazzling display of a fabulous jewelry store, but there is no soft grass to sit upon, no green trees to enjoy and no water to drink or food to eat. However, here introduced are the elements which add a rich softness to this city of elaborate beauty.

There was a river in the first Eden which branched into four rivers; although there was abundance of water it is not called the water of life. Eden was a garden of trees among which was the tree of life. (God kept the way open for man by the shedding of blood, see Gen. 3:24.)

In the New Jerusalem there is a river of the water of life, and the throne of God is its living fountain supplying an abundance of water.

The *tree of life* is a fruit tree, bearing twelve kinds of fruit each month. There is a continuous supply in abundance and variety. In eternity man will eat and drink. The menu is varied but is restricted to fruits, as it was in the Garden of Eden.

> And God said, Behold, I have given you every herb bearing seed, which is upon the face of all the earth, and every tree, in the which is the fruit of a tree yielding seed; to you it shall be for meat. And to every beast of the earth, and to every fowl of the air, and to every thing that creepeth upon the earth, wherein there is life, I have given every green herb for meat: and it was so (Gen. 1:29, 30).

Even the leaves of the tree are beneficial. They have a medicinal value. Why is healing needed in a perfect universe? This is a difficult problem. Perhaps it is a first aid kit which demonstrates the old adage, "an ounce of prevention is worth a pound of cure." Also, perhaps the bodies of the earth dwellers will need renewing from time to time.

Verses 3-5—And there shall be no more curse: but the throne of God and of the Lamb shall be in it; and his servants shall serve him: And they shall see his face; and his name shall be in their foreheads. And there shall be no night there; and they need no candle, neither light of the sun; for the Lord God giveth them light: and they shall reign for ever and ever.

And there shall be no curse anymore: and the throne of God and of the Lamb shall be therein: and his servants shall do him service: and they shall see his face; and his name shall be on their foreheads. All there shall be night no more; and they need no light of lamp, neither light of sun; for the Lord God shall give them light: and they shall reign for ever and ever.

The first creation was blighted by the curse of sin. This old earth on which we live bears many scar-marks of the curse of sin. The new creation will never be marred by sin. Sin will never be permitted to enter even potentially. The very presence of God and the Lamb will be adequate to prevent it. It was during the absence of God in the Garden of Eden that the tempter came to our first parents.

The New Jerusalem will be GHQ for God the Father and God the Son. The notable absence of any reference to the Holy Spirit needs some explanation. In the first creation the Holy Spirit came after the fall to renovate and renew the blighted creation. There will be no need of His work in the new creation. The silence of God at this point is eloquent.

And his servants shall do him service reveals that heaven is not a place of unoccupied idleness, but is a place of ceaseless activity. It will not be necessary to rest in order to give the body an opportunity to recuperate. The word for *service* has a peculiar usage. Vincent says, "It came to be used by the Jews in a very special sense, to denote the service rendered to Jehovah by the Israelites as His peculiar people" (see Heb. 9:1, 6).

There will be ceaseless activity, since there is no night. Man will at last fulfill his destiny and satisfy the desires of his heart.

Man will at last see His face. This was the supreme desire voiced by Moses and Philip. It is the highest objective for living. What divine satisfaction!

Each person will bear the name of Christ: each will be like Him—yet without disturbing his own peculiar personality.

Again in this section our attention is called to the direct lighting of the new creation. There will be no light holders, such as the sun, or reflectors, such as the moon. God lights the universe by His presence, for God is light.

It is in eternity that the Church shall reign with Christ. Who knows but what He will give to each saint a world or solar system or galactic system to operate. Remember that Adam was given dominion over the old creation.

7. Promise of the Return of Christ, verses 6-16

Verses 6,7—And he said unto me, These sayings are faithful and true: and the Lord God of the holy prophets sent his angel to shew unto his servants the things which must shortly be done. Behold, I come quickly: blessed is he that keepeth the sayings of the prophecy of this book.

And he said unto me, These words are faithful and true: and the Lord, the God of the spirits of the prophets, sent his angel to show unto his servants the things which must shortly come to pass. And behold, I come quickly. Blessed is he that keepeth the words of the prophecy of this book.

Verse 6 through to the end of the chapter, gives the conclusion of this book. Verse 5 brought to an end the revelation of Jesus Christ. When the Church is dwelling with Him in the fulness of the light of His presence, and is reigning with Him, He will be satisfied. The far-off purpose of all creation is finally accomplished. This is the *pleroma* of the revelation of Jesus Christ.

The Lord Jesus puts His own seal upon this book.

The words are faithful and true, which means that no man is to trifle with them by spiritualizing them or reducing them to meaningless symbols.

In the introduction to this book a blessing is pronounced upon those who read, and hear, and keep these words. In conclusion, the Lord Jesus repeats the blessing upon those who keep these words. This is a book to not merely satisfy the curiosity of the natural man, but to live and act upon. This is most solemn.

The Lord God thought it important enough to send His angel to reveal future events. No true minister of the Word can ignore prophecy.

The Lord Jesus repeats the promise, with which He opened this book, that He was coming quickly (rapidly). This promise is repeated three times in this conclusion (verses 7, 12, 20). This threefold repetition reveals that the return of Christ is all important to God. It should be so to us.

Verses 8-11—And I John saw these things, and heard them. And when I had heard and seen, I fell down to worship before the feet of the angel which shewed me these things. Then saith he unto me, See thou do it not: for I am thy fellowservant, and of thy brethren the prophets, and of them which keep the sayings of this book: worship God. And he saith unto me, Seal not the sayings of the prophecy of this book: for the time is at hand. He that is un-

just, let him be unjust still: and he which is filthy, let him be filthy still: and he that is righteous, let him be righteous still: and he that is holy, let him be holy still.

And I John am he that heard and saw these things. And when I heard and saw, I fell down to worship before the feet of the angel that showed me these things. And he saith unto me, See (thou do it) not: I am a fellow servant with thee and with thy brethren the prophets, and with them that keep the words of this book: worship God. And he saith unto me, Seal not up the words of the prophecy of this book; for the time is at hand. He that is unrighteous, let him do unrighteousness still; and he that is filthy, let him me made filthy still: and he that is righteous, let him do righteousness still: and he that is holy let him be made holy still.

This is John's final and oft repeated statement that he was both auditor and spectator to the scenes in the book. This is the method that was put down at the very opening of this book (see Revelation 1:1). This is the first T.V. program. God used both the eye gate and ear gate to convey to John the messages of this book—their profundity and importance demanded it.

John was so impressed that his natural reaction was to fall down and worship the angel. The simplicity and meekness of the angel are impressive. Though the angels were created above man, this angel identifies himself as a fellow servant with John and the other prophets. He was merely a messenger to communicate God's Word to man. He directs all worship to God.

Daniel was told to seal up the words of his prophecy because of the long interval before the fulfillment of it.

> But thou, O Daniel, shut up the words, and seal the book, even to the time of the end: many shall run to and fro, and knowledge shall be increased (Dan. 12:4).

In contrast, the prophecy given to John was even then in process of being fulfilled. For 1900 years the Church has been passing through the time periods of the seven churches given in chapters 2 and 3.

Probably the most frightful condition of the lost is revealed here, even more so than at the Great White Throne Judgment of chapter 20. The sinful condition of the lost is a permanent and eternal thing; although it is not static, for the suggestion is that the unrighteous will increasingly become more unrighteous the filthy "will be made filthy still." The condition of the lost gets worse until each becomes a monster of sin. This thought is frightful.

On the other hand, neither is the condition of the servant of God static. They will continue to grow in righteousness and holiness. Heaven is not static. Even in the Millennium "of the increase of his kingdom there shall be no end." What a glorious and engaging prospect this should be for the child of God! We shall have all eternity to grow and know.

Verses 12-16—And, behold, I come quickly; and my reward is with me, to give every man according as his work shall be. I am Alpha and Omega, the beginning and the end, the first and the last. Blessed are they that do his commandments, that they may have right to the tree of life, and may enter in through the gates into the city. For without are dogs, and sorcerers, and

94

whoremongers, and murderers, and idolaters, and whosoever loveth and maketh a lie. I Jesus have sent mine angel to testify unto you these things in the churches. I am the root and the offspring of David, and the bright and morning star.

Behold, I come quickly; and my reward is with me, to render to each man according as his work is. I am the Alpha and the Omega, the first and the last, the beginning and the end. Blessed are they that wash their robes, in order that theirs shall be authority over the tree of life, and may enter by the gates into the city. Without are the dogs, and the sorcerers, and the fornicators, and the murderers, and the idolaters, and every one that loveth and maketh a lie. I Jesus have sent mine angel to testify unto you these things for the churches. I am the root and the offspring of David, the bright, the morning star.

Either the angel is bearing this very personal word from Jesus, or the Lord breaks through and speaks personally.

He promises that He is coming again. This is His personal declaration. No believer can doubt or deny this all-important and personal promise of the Lord Jesus.

He will personally reward each believer individually—the Church at the rapture, and Israel and the Gentiles at His return to set up His kingdom at the Millennium. Little wonder that Paul exclaimed,

That I may know him, and the power of his resurrection, and the fellowship of his sufferings, being made conformable unto his death; if by any means I might attain unto the resurrection of the dead. Not as though I had already attained, either were already perfect: but I follow after, if that I may apprehend that for which also I am apprehended of Christ Jesus. Brethren, I count not myself to have apprehended: but this one thing I do, forgetting those things which are behind, and reaching forth unto those things which are before, I press toward the mark for the prize of the high calling of God in Christ Jesus (Phil. 3:10-14).

Again He asserts His deity—"I am Alpha and Omega, the first and the last the beginning and the end" (see Revelation 1:8).

Only blood-washed believers have authority over the tree of life and access to the holy city (see Ephesians 1:7-12).

Dogs come off rather badly in Scripture. This perhaps does not mean that there will be no dogs in heaven; but because dogs were scavengers in the ancient world, they were considered unclean and impure. (See Matthew 15:21-28 where "dogs" was the designation for Gentiles; and Philippians 3:2 where "dogs" is Paul's label for Judaizers.)

Again we are reminded that there is a great gulf fixed between lost and saved.

Apparently the Lord Jesus had sent His angel with this very personal message.

I Jesus . . . He takes the name of His saviourhood, the name He received when He took our humanity—*Jesus*.

That at the name of Jesus every knee should bow, of things in

heaven, and things in earth, and things under the earth (Phil. 2:10).
The name Jesus speaks of His first coming.

He is the root and the offspring of David (see Isa. 11:1; 4:2; Jer. 23:5; 33:15; and Zech. 3:8). These references speak of His coming as king.

He is *the bright, the morning star* to the Church, for He appears in the pre-dawn darkness to take the Church out of the world. Then He will come as "the Sun of righteousness."

> But unto you that fear my name shall the Sun of righteousness arise with healing in his wings; and ye shall go forth, and grow up as calves of the stall (Mal. 4:2).

8. Final Invitation and Warning, verses 17-19

Verses 17-19—And the Spirit and the bride say, Come. And let him that heareth say, Come. And let him that is athirst come. And whosoever will, let him take the water of life freely. For I testify unto every man that heareth the words of the prophecy of this book, If any man shall add unto these things, God shall add unto him the plagues that are written in this book: and if any man shall take away from the words of the book of this prophecy, God shall take away his part out of the book of life, and out of the holy city, and from the things which are written in this book.

And the Spirit and the bride say, Come. And he that heareth, let him say, Come. And he that is athirst, let him come: he that will, let him take the water of life freely. I testify unto every man that heareth the words of the prophecy of this book, If any man shall add unto them, God shall add the plagues which are written in this book: and if any man shall take away from the words of the book of this prophecy, God shall take away his part from the tree of life, and out of the holy city, which are written in this book.

The Holy Spirit is in the world today and He joins in prayer through the Church to petition the Lord to come. This is the blessed hope of the Church; and only the Holy Spirit can make it vital, real, and important to the believer. Even the one hearing this book of the Revelation should join the prayer meeting to pray for Him to come.

The Holy Spirit is performing His ministry in the world today of convicting and converting men. He works through the Word and through the Church which proclaims His Word, urging men to come to Christ that they might be saved, in view of the Coming of Christ and the certainty of judgment (see John 16:7-11; Acts 24:25; Ephesians 1:13).

The Spirit and the bride say, Come is an invitation to men to take the water of life freely.

> Ho, every one that thirsteth, come ye to the waters, and he that hath no money; come ye, buy, and eat; yea, come, buy wine and milk without money and without price (Isa. 55:1).
>
> In the last day, that great day of the feast, Jesus stood and cried, saying, If any man thirst, let him come unto me, and drink (John 7:37).

After this follows a solemn word of warning to any who would trifle with the words of this book. Let modern theologians ponder these words when they seek to minimize the importance of this book. Let the modern preacher, who refuses to preach and teach this book, consider these words. Let all beware that they add not or subtract not from the words of this book. The words are to be taken seriously and literally.

9. Final Promise and Prayer, verses 20, 21

Verses 20, 21—He which testifieth these things saith, Surely I come quickly. Amen. Even so, come, Lord Jesus. The grace of our Lord Jesus Christ be with you all. Amen.

He who testifieth these things saith, Yea: I come quickly. Amen: Come, Lord Jesus. The grace of the Lord Jesus be with all the saints. Amen.

This is the final postscript of the Lord Jesus. He signed it personally, for He is the Amen.

> And unto the angel of the church of the Laodiceans write; These things saith the Amen, the faithful and true witness, the beginning of the creation of God (Rev. 3:14).

> For all the promises of God in him are yea, and in him Amen, unto the glory of God by us (II Cor. 1:20).

This is His third and final declaration that He is coming. He is saying, "Yes, I am coming." Do you believe Him?

The heart cry of every true believer is, *Come.*

The Old Testament ends with a curse: the New Testament ends with a benediction of grace upon the believers. Grace is offered to all. But if any man refuses the offer, which is extended regardless of merit, he must bear the judgment pronounced in this book.

Grace is still offered to man. It is God's method of saving sinners.

> For by grace are ye saved through faith; and that not of yourselves: it is the gift of God: not of works, lest any man should boast (Eph. 2:8, 9).

Amazing grace! how sweet the sound,
That saved a wretch like me!
I once was lost, but now am found,
Was blind, but now I see.

—John Newton

APPENDIX

THE SHAPE OF THINGS TO COME

This is a consideration of the apocalyptic city as seen by the seer on the island of Patmos. She is seen in the lovely figure of a bride adorned for her husband. The appearance of this city is the quintessence of beauty, refined loveliness, and uncontrolled joy. Lofty language describes her merits, and descriptive vocabulary is exhausted in painting her portrait. The contemplation of her coming glory is a spiritual tonic for those who grow weary on the pilgrim journey.

The New Jerusalem is a post-millennial city, for she does not come into view until the end of the Millennium and the beginning of eternity.[1] This city was evidently in the mind of Christ when He said, "I go to prepare a place for you." The curtain does not rise upon the scene of the heavenly city until earth's drama has reached a satisfactory conclusion. Earth's sorrow is not hushed until the endless ages begin.

The New Jerusalem will be to eternity what the earthly Jerusalem is to the Millennium. The earthly Jerusalem does not pass away but it takes second place in eternity. Righteousness *reigns* in Jerusalem, it will *dwell* in the New Jerusalem. Imperfection and rebellion exist even in the Millennial Jerusalem; perfection and the absence of sin will identify the heavenly city. Just as a king's queen is of more importance than the place of his government, thus the New Jerusalem transcends the city of earth. This will cast no reflection on the earthly city nor will it cause her inward pain. She can say in the spirit of John the Baptist, "She that hath the bridegroom is the bride."

The New Jerusalem is the eternal abode of the Church. The New Jerusalem is the home of the Church—the home town of the Church. She is a city toward which the Church is journeying as she pitches her tent in that direction. We are now to look at this new home by reading the architect's blueprint in Revelation, the 21st chapter.

Verse 1—A New Heaven and a New Earth

The landscape about the heavenly Jerusalem is different from that of the earthly city. It is a new heaven and a new earth that is before us. There is no parallel for this in Scripture. It does not say that there is a destruction of the earth and the creation of another earth. Nor does it intimate that it is a repetition of Genesis 1:2 where it is evident that this earth suffered some catastrophic judgment and "became without form and void (*tohu va bohu*)." The six days of creation were actually days of redecoration, rearranging, refurnishing, and replenishing. However, a new heaven and a new earth suggest that this preparation for the eternal existence of the earth is more far reaching in extent than anything preceding it. One example will indicate the extent of these changes. It is declared in this same verse "and there was no more sea." That which covers more than two-thirds of the earth's surface will be removed. The sea is responsible for life on this earth in an indirect way. It furnishes rainfall, food, and an avenue of transportation. Its importance to the maintenance of life can-

---

[1] Lange's Commentary, p. 390.

not be over emphasized. Its influence upon life cannot be overlooked. The politics of nations are shaped largely by their geographical relationship to the sea. Yet in the eternal state there will be no more sea. It is impossible for us to conceive of this change, yet we readily see that it will be a radical departure from our present arrangement.

Verse 2—A Bride Adorned for Her Husband

A woman may not be very pretty before her wedding and after it, but there is one time when every woman is lovely—at her wedding. The city that now comes before us is "as a bride adorned for her husband." There is no question regarding the genuine loveliness and beauty of this bride. The bridegroom has seen to it, "That he might present it to himself, a glorious church, not having spot, or wrinkle, or any such thing; but that it should be holy and without blemish" (Eph. 5:27). The vision of the seer on Patmos, with the language of inspiration, exhausts the vocabulary of heaven in describing the glories of this bride-city. As a lovely bride turns from the altar of marriage and proceeds in stately beauty, radiant with youthful ecstasy, so the virgin bride of Christ comes forth from heaven, in pristine beauty, prepared to enjoy eternal fellowship with her Lord.

Verse 9—"Come hither, I will show thee the bride, the Lamb's wife."

What follows is a description of the city. We must pause here to consider the relationship of the city to the citizens—the city proper to the Church. Certainly we are not to infer that the empty city without the citizens is the bride. The citizens are identified with the city in Revelation 22:3, 6, 19. Those outside are identified in Revelation 21:8 as disfranchised. Although a distinction between the Bride and the city needs to be maintained, it is the intent of the writer to consider them together. This passage is a description of the adornments which reveal something of the love and worth that the bridegroom has conferred upon her.

Verse 10—"That great city, the holy Jerusalem, descending out of heaven from God"

Certainly this city has no counterpart among earth's cities. They are built upon an earthly foundation and come up from the bottom. This city comes down out of heaven. She originates in heaven, and God is her architect and builder. Although the city comes down out of heaven, there is no suggestion that she comes down to the earth. The earthly city never goes to heaven, and the heavenly city never comes to earth. Just how far down the city descends is a matter of speculation. This has led to extreme views in interpreting the New Jerusalem. Ebionism (one of the first heresies) went to one extreme in applying this whole passage concerning the New Jerusalem to the earthly Jerusalem. The Gnostics (another early heresy) went to the other extremity in spirtualizing the passage to make it refer to heaven. Many modern isms apply the New Jerusalem to themselves and set it up on earth at the geographic location of their choice. Liberal theologians and amillenarians have left the city in heaven in spite of the Scriptural statement that it comes down "out of heaven."

Two facts are evident from this passage. (1) It comes down out of heaven; (2) and it is not stated that it comes to the earth. The passage of Scripture leaves the city hanging in mid air. That is the dilemma that many seek to avoid—but why not leave the city in mid air? Is there anything incongruous about a civilization in space? The New Jerusalem will either become another satellite to the earth; or, what is more probable, the earth will become a satellite to the New Jerusalem. This chapter indicates that the city be the center of things. All activity and glory revolve about this city. God will be there, it will be His headquarters, and His universe is theocentric. The New Jerusalem is therefore worthy to merit such a preeminent position for eternity.

Verse 11—"Having the glory of God: and her light was like unto a stone most precious, even like a jasper stone, clear as crystal"

Paul instructs the believers to "rejoice in hope of the glory of God" (Rom. 5:2). This hope will be realized in the holy city. Man in sin has never witnessed the revelation of the glory of God. The experience of Israel in the wilderness taught them that each time there was rebellion in the camp, the glory of God appeared in judgment. The manifestation of God's glory strikes terror to a sinful heart. But what glorious anticipation to be able to behold His glory when standing clothed in the righteousness of Christ! Two wonderful facts make this city the manifestation of the fulness of God's glory. (1) The presence of God makes the city the source of glory for the universe. Every blessing radiates from this city. (2) The presence of the saints do not forbid the manifestation of the glory of God. Sin caused God to remove His glory from man's presence. In this city all that is past. Redeemed man dwelling with God in a city "having the glory of God" is the grand goal which is worthy of God. This city reveals the high purpose of God in the Church which is to bring "many sons to glory."

The word translated light (*phoster*) is the word for source of light. The city is a light giver. It does not reflect light as the moon, nor does it generate light by physical combustion like the sun, but it originates light and is the source of light. The presence of God and Christ give explanation to this as He declared, "I am the light. . . ."

The whole city is like a precious gem. This gem is likened unto the jasper stone. The modern jasper is multi-colored quartz stone. The stone referred to here cannot be that, for this stone is not opaque. Jasper is a transliteration of the word *iaspis* which is of Semetic origin. Moffatt suggests that *iaspis* could mean the modern opal, diamond, or topaz.

The stone is "transparent and gleaming" which suggests one of these stones, most likely the diamond. The diamond seems to fit the description better than any other stone known to man. The similarity of the Hebrew word for crystal in Ezekiel 1:22 to the Hebrew word for ice helps to strengthen this view. The New Jerusalem is a diamond in a gold mounting. This city is the engagement ring of the Bride—it is the symbol of the betrothal of the Church to Christ.

Verses 12-13, 17-18—The Wall and the Gates

The wall of a city is for protection. A walled city is a safe city. The New Jerusalem is safe and those who dwell therein dwell in safety. The heavenly Salem will enjoy the fruits of safety and peace. Made up of those who found peace with God on earth, she will experience the fulness of peace throughout eternity. The walls are a sign that this city has achieved the full meaning of her name.

The walls are 144 cubits in height or about 216 feet. Herodotus gives the estimation for the walls of ancient Babylon as 50 cubits thick and 200 cubits high. These walls were built to make the city impregnable. The great height of the walls of the New Jerusalem are but commensurate with the great size of the city. Beauty rather than protection is the motive in design. It is a wall with jasper built into it, and is generally designated a jasper wall. The hardest of substances and the most beautiful gem constitutes the exterior of the city.

There are twelve gates to this city, three gates on each side. On each gate is the name of one of the tribes of Israel. This is very striking and suggests immediately the order of the children of Israel about the tabernacle. The tribe of Levi, as the priesthood, served in the tabernacle proper. The New Jerusalem is a temple or tabernacle in one sense, for God is there dwelling with man. The Church constitutes the priesthood who serve Him constantly. They serve as such in the city and dwell there as did Levi about the tabernacle. Everything in eternity will face in toward this city, for God is there. The children of Israel on earth will enjoy the same relationship to this city that they did toward the wilderness tabernacle and later the city temple. This city will be a tabernacle to Israel. The children of Israel will be among the multitudes who come into this city to worship in eternity. They will come from the earth to bring their worship and glory. They will not dwell in the city any more than they dwelt in the tabernacle of old. Those who actually dwell there will be the priests, who are the Church. The Church occupies the closer place to God in eternity. The Bride, like John in the upper room, reclines upon His breast. "Who is this that cometh up from the wilderness, leaning upon her beloved?" asks the Song of Solomon. She is the Bride and she has come up from the wilderness which is this present world. But the 12 tribes of Israel will come up to the celestial city to worship, three tribes coming up on each of the four sides.

Verse 21—"The twelve gates were twelve pearls"

The coat of arms of the New Jerusalem is the pearl. Each gate is one pearl and the one entering the city is confronted by this seal of identification. This mark is in full accord with the Scriptural identification of those who dwell therein. The Church is set forth by Christ in parabolic form as the "pearl of great price." In the Bible the Church has no name. The date of her birth was not given beforehand (five minutes before the Holy Spirit came on the day of Pentecost we have no reason to believe that anyone knew that there would be a Church that day). Likewise, there is no date given for the *parousia*, the rapture, of the Church. Although the Church is called the Bride of Christ, she has no name or age recorded. However, if the "pearl of great price" which was sought by the merchant man is the Church, then it is interesting to note the word for pearl. In the Greek text the word is *margarites*, which can be easily transliterated *Margaret*. Could this be the name of the Church?

The parable of the pearl of great price is given in Matthew 13:45, 46.

> Again, the kingdom of heaven is like unto a merchant man, seeking goodly pearls: who, when he had found one pearl of great price, went and sold all that he had, and bought it.

The hero is the merchant man. He cannot be the sinner seeking Christ. The sinner is not found seeking Christ; the contrary is true—Christ is seeking the sinner. If a sinner were seeking Christ, he could not buy Him, for He is not for sale—"God so loved the world that *he gave* his only begotten son." The merchant man is described as selling all that he had. What has a sinner to sell that would furnish legal tender in heaven when "the righteousness of man is filthy rags?" This interpretation breaks down at every point. Actually, Christ is the merchant man seeking goodly pearls. He came from afar, having left heaven to come to earth. He found one pearl of great price, the Church. He saw her as she would be, complete and faultless before Him. He went and sold all that he had, as Paul phrases it, "for our sakes he became poor." At a high cost He purchased the Pearl, "for ye are bought with a price," and that price is defined by Peter, "ye were not redeemed with corruptible things, as silver and gold, from your vain conversation received by tradition from your fathers; but with the precious blood of Christ, as of a lamb without blemish and without spot" (I Pet. 1:18, 19).

The pearl is the only precious gem that is not a stone. All others are mineral, but the pearl is formed by an organism which lives in the sea. A living organism is wounded by the intrusion of a piece of sand or other defilement. It throws off a fluid that completely covers the grain of sand. Again and again it sends forth this liquid until one layer after another is added and the pearl is formed. The organism forms the pearl out of itself, for the grain of sand is not the pearl.

The Church is God's answer to sin. Someone has said that we got into the heart of Christ through a spear wound. The Church is made up of sinners. These sinners caused Christ to die, but His answer to the grain of sin was to cover the sinner with the spotless robe of His righteousness. He paid the penalty for sin that He might present us faultless before the throne of His presence. The Bride is the pearl of great price and she is being formed as a pearl is formed. It is in keeping with the origin of the Church that the gates to her abode should be of pearl. The pearl sets forth not only the manner in which the Church is formed, but the foundation which is the blood of Christ, the most precious thing about the New Jerusalem.

Verse 14—The Foundations

This city has twelve foundations and the names of the twelve apostles are upon them. The church is "built upon the foundation of the apostles and prophets, Jesus Christ himself being the chief corner stone" (Eph. 2:20). When Christ returned to heaven, He committed the keys into the keeping of the apostles; on the human level the church was in the hands of these twelve men. The book of Acts gives the order, "The former treatise have I made, O Theophilus, of all that *Jesus began* both to do and teach, until the day in which he was taken up, after that *he through the Holy Ghost* had given commandments unto the *apostles whom he had chosen*" (Acts 1:1, 2).

Who was the twelfth apostle to take the place of Judas? Certainly the election which Simon Peter conducted among the apostles for a twelfth did not give their candidate enough prestige to have even his name mentioned again. Though a fine, noble Christian, he was not the choice of the Holy Spirit for this high office. However, Saul of Tarsus, arrested by the Lord on the Damascus Road, was given the title of apostle and also given the evidence and credentials that went with the office—that of being a witness of the resurrected Lord. With divine authority he writes, "Paul, an apostle, (not of men, neither by man, but by Jesus Christ, and God the Father, who raised him from the dead;)" (Gal. 1:11).

To these twelve apostles were committed all the writings of the church. These men preached the first sermons, organized the first churches, and became the first martyrs. It is not honoring to Scripture to attempt to minimize the importance of the twelve apostles. In a real sense they were the foundation of the church. To them the church shall be eternally grateful—and this is not to rob Christ of His place, for He is "the chief corner stone." But the Church is "built upon the foundation of the apostles and prophets."

Verses 19, 20—The Stones of Fire in the Foundation

These twelve foundations not only have the names of the twelve apostles but are twelve different precious stones. The most beautiful and costly articles known to man are precious stones. These stones express in human terms the magnificence of the city. The superlative degree of gems is used to convey something of the glory of this city to those who now "see through a glass darkly." A close examination of the twelve stones in the foundation reveal a polychromed paragon of beauty; varied hues and tints form a galaxy of rainbow colors. The stones are enumerated as follows:

1. Jasper, (*iaspis*). Color: clear.
   As mentioned aforetime, this is the diamond. It is crystal clear, a reflector of light and color. Dr. Seiss in speaking of the New Jerusalem describes it "as clean, and pure, and bright as a transparent icicle in the sunshine."

2. Sapphire (*sappheiros*). Color: blue.
   This stone occurs in Exodus 24:10 as the foundation of God, "and there was under his feet as it were a paved work of a sapphire stone, and as it were the body of heaven in his clearness." Moffatt describes it as a blue stone. Pliny describes it as opaque with gold specks, to which Petrie agrees.

3. Chalcedony (*chalkedon*). Color: greenish.
   Agate. Pliny describes it as "a variety of emerald gathered on a mountain in Chalcedon." Robertson says, "Possibly a green silicate of copper."

4. Emerald (*smaragdos*). Color: green.
   Robertson describes it as a green stone.

5. Sardonyx (*sardonux*). Color: red.
   Robertson describes it as white with layers of red.

6. Sardius (*sardios*). Color: fiery red.
   Pliny says that it is a red stone from Sardis. Swete says that it is fiery red.

7. Chrysolyte (*chrusolithos*). Color: golden yellow.
   Moffatt assigns it a golden hue; Robertson says it is a golden color like our topaz.

8. Beryl (*berullos*). Color: Sea green.
   Sea green of Pliny's time. Like the emerald, says Robertson.

9. Topaz (*topazion*). Color: greenish yellow.
   Robertson calls it a golden greenish stone.

10. Chrysoprasus (*chrusoprasos*). Color: gold-green.
    A golden leek, "a leek colored gem," says Robertson. The I.S.B.E. lists it as sea green.

11. Jacinth (*huakinthi*). Color: violet.

Color of the hyacinth. Pliny gives the color as violet.

12. Amethyst (*amethustos*). Color: purple.

Although the I.S.B.E. lists it as a ruby, Robertson gives the color as purple. The foundations of the New Jerusalem are constructed of the flashing brilliance of rich and costly gems.

Color is described as dissected light. Pass a ray of light through a prism and it is broken up into three primary colors: red, blue, yellow. From these three primary colors come all colors and shades of colors. Light is a requirement for color. Where there is no light, there is no color. Objects of color reveal color to the eye because of their ability to absorb or reject light rays. A red stone absorbs all the color rays except red, it rejects or throws back to the eye the red ray, which gives it the color of red. The New Jerusalem is a city of light and a city of color. "God is light" and He is there. The city is described as a jasper stone and clear as crystal. The jasper stone is a sphere and the city, New Jerusalem, is within. The light shining from within through the jasper stone, acting as a prism, would give every color and shade of color in the rainbow city of Jerusalem. The New Jerusalem is a new planet, as we shall see, and the city is inside a crystal ball. The presence of the primary colors suggests that every shade and tint is reflected from that city. A rainbow that appears after a summer shower gives only a faint impression of the beauty in coloring of the city of light.

Verses 15, 16—The Size and Shape of the City

The measurements of the city have given rise to all sorts of conceptions as to the size and shape of the city. First of all, let us examine the size of the city. Twelve thousand furlongs are given as the measurement of each side and height. It is 12,000 *stadia* in the text, which means about 1500 miles. This figure is corroborated by Dr. Seiss, Walter Scott, and others. The amplitude of the city is astounding when first considered, but is commensurate with the importance of the city. Certainly God as creator can never be accused of stinting, economizing, or doing things that reveal littleness. With a lavish hand He garnished the heavens with stellar bodies. This city bears the trade mark of its maker.

Now consider with me the shape of the city. "The city lieth foursquare" is the simple declaration of Scripture. That would seem to indicate that the city is a cube with 1500 miles on a side—1500 miles long, 1500 miles wide, and 1500 miles high. Dr. Seiss sees it as a cube. Dr. Harry Ironside sees it as a pyramid. Still others interpret these measurements in as many geometric figures. However it is difficult to conceive of either a cube or pyramid projected out in space. We are accustomed to think of a sphere hanging in space because that is the general shape of heavenly bodies. Cubes and pyramids are appropriate for earth's buildings, but are impracticable for space, as spheres are impracticable for earthly buildings. Yet it is definitely stated that the city is foursquare.

The difficulty resolves when we think of the city as a cube within a crystal clear sphere. Several times attention is called to the fact that the city is like a crystal-clear stone or crystal-clear gold. This emphasis leads us to believe that

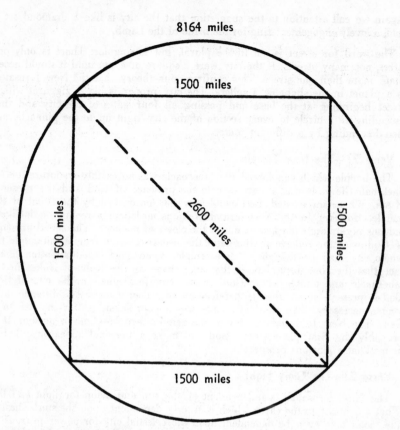

8164 miles

1500 miles

1500 miles

1500 miles

2600 miles

1500 miles

Size of the city inside crystal sphere equals 1500 miles on each side.
Diameter of the sphere equals 2600 miles
Circumference of the sphere equals 8164 miles.

the city is seen through the crystal. We live on the *outside* of the planet called earth, but the Bride will dwell *within* the planet called the New Jerusalem. The glory of light streaming through this crystal-clear prism, will break up into a polychromed rainbow of breath-taking beauty. The sphere will have the circumference of 8164 miles. The diameter of the moon is about 2,160 miles, and that of the New Jerusalem sphere is about 2,600 miles; thus the New Jerusalem will be about the size of the moon. And it will be a sphere, as are the other heavenly bodies.

Verses 18 and 21—The City and Street of Gold

Man has perfected through processes of metallurgy different colors of gold—yellow, green, white gold; but we are not yet seeing transparent gold. However the gold of the New Jerusalem is like clear glass. The city is translucent but the material is gold in contrast to the crystal-clear stone that surrounds the city.

Again we call attention to the suggestion that the city is like a diamond set in gold, a lovely engagement ring for the bride of the Lamb.

The word for street is not in the plural, but is singular. There is only one street, not many streets. If the city were a square or a pyramid it would necessitate more than one street. This confirms our theory that the New Jerusalem is a planet in the shape of a sphere. The city proper is like a ziggurat with a street beginning at the base and passing all four gates of the city and then ascending in a circle to every section of the city right up to the pinnacle, and then descending by a different route.

Verse 22—The New Temple

The temple which supplanted the tabernacle was an earthly enclosure for the Shekinah Glory. It was a testimony to the presence of God and the presence of sin. Where sin existed, God could only be approached by the ritual of the temple. However in the New Jerusalem sin is no longer a reality—it is like a hideous nightmare even locked out of the closet of memory. The actual presence of God with the redeemed eliminates the necessity for a temple, although the whole city may be thought of as a temple. Some have called attention to the fact that the New Jerusalem is the same shape as the Holy of Holies in the tabernacle and temple where God dwelt—a perfect cube. In the city of light God is present, sin is absent, therefore an edifice of a material substance is no longer necessary. The physical temple was a poor substitute for the person of God. The New Jerusalem possesses the genuine article—God in person. It is probably the first place where God will make a personal appearance before man. What a glorious prospect!

Verse 23—The Glory Light

The New Jerusalem is independent of the sun and moon for light and life. What a contrast to the earth which is utterly dependent upon the sun! The sun and moon may even be dependent upon the celestial city for power to transmit light, since the One who is the source of light and life dwells within the city. Neither will light be furnished by the New Jerusalem Power and Light Company. The One who is light will be there, and the effulgence of His glory will be manifested in the New Jerusalem unhindered.

Verses 24-27—The Cosmopolitan City

Attention already has been directed to the fact that a redeemed remnant of Israel makes regular visits to this city of God. In verse 24 another group is identified who come into the city to bring their glory and honor. These are the redeemed Gentile nations who will occupy the earth together with Israel for eternity. These nations, like Israel, do not belong to the Church for they are redeemed after the Church is removed from the earth. They come as visitors to the city. In Hebrews 12:22 we are told that there is also present an innumerable company of angels who evidently constitute the servant class. The city is cosmopolitan in character. All nationalities meet there and the created intelligences of God walk the street of the New Jerusalem. Among the multitudes there is not one who will bring defilement or sin. How superior is this city to the Garden of Eden where the lie of Satan made an entree for sin! No lie or liar will ever enter the portals of the heavenly Jerusalem. All dwellers and all

tourists are not only redeemed from sin, but have lost their taste for sin. They
come through its gates which are never closed. The enjoyment of this glorious
city is not restricted to the Church, although they are the only ones who dwell
there.

> Jerusalem, the golden, with milk and honey blest!
> Beneath thy contemplation sink heart and voice oppressed;
> I know not, O I know not what joys await me there;
> What radiancy of glory, what bliss beyond compare.
>
> —*Bernard of Cluny*

BIBLIOGRAPHY

RECOMMENDED BOOKS

Govett, Robert. *The Apocalypse Expounded by Scripture.* London: Thyme, 1922.

Ironside, H.A. *Lectures on the Book of Revelation.* Neptune, New Jersey: Loizeaux 1960.

Lindsay, Hal. *There's a New World Coming.* Santa Ana, California: Vision Hou Publishers, 1973.

Newell, William R. *The Book of Revelation.* Chicago: Moody Press, 1935.

Ryrie, Charles C. *Revelation.* Chicago: Moody Press, 1968. (A fine, inexpensive surve of the book.)

Scott, Walter. *Exposition of the Revelation of Jesus Christ.* London: Pickering ar Inglis, n.d.

Seiss, J.A. *The Apocalypse, Lectures on the Book of Revelation.* Grand Rapids: Zonde van, 1957.

Smith, J.B. *A Revelation of Jesus Christ.* Scottsdale, Pennsylvania: Herald Press, 196

Strauss, Lehman. *The Book of Revelation.* Neptune, New Jersey: Loizeaux, 1964.

Walvoord, John F. *The Revelation of Jesus Christ.* Chicago: Moody Press, 1966.

HELPFUL BOOKS ON BIBLE PROPHECY

Hoyt, Herman A. *The End Times.* Chicago: Moody Press, 1969.

Pentecost, J. Dwight. *Things to Come.* Grand Rapids: Dunham, 1958.

Pentecost, J. Dwight. *Prophecy For Today.* Grand Rapids: Zondervan, 1961.

Pentecost, J. Dwight. *Will Man Survive?* Chicago: Moody Press, 1971.

Ryrie, Charles C. *The Basis of the Premillennial Faith.* Neptune, New Jersey: Loizeau 1953.

Ryrie, Charles C. *The Bible and Tomorrow's News.* Wheaton, Illinois: Scripture Pr Publications, 1969.

Unger, Merrill F. *Beyond the Crystal Ball.* Chicago: Moody Press, 1973.

Walvoord, John F. *Armageddon, Oil and the Middle East Crisis.* Grand Rapids: Zond van, 1974.

Walvoord, John F. *The Blessed Hope and the Tribulation.* Grand Rapids: Zonderva 1976.

Walvoord, John F. *The Millennial Kingdom.* Grand Rapids: Dunham, 1959.

Thru The Bible Books

P. O. Box 100   •   Pasadena, California 91109

Touchinglives.org
800-413-1131
@touchinglivestv
Facebook.com/TLonFB